Offbeats

Lower East Side Portraits

Clayton Patterson & John Strausbaugh

Copyright © 2022 by Clayton Patterson and John Strausbaugh

Cool Grove Press is an imprint of Cool Grove Publishing, Inc., New York.
512 Argyle Road, Brooklyn, NY 11218

All rights reserved under the International and
Pan-American Copyright Conventions. https://coolgrove.com/books

[For permissions and other inquiries write to info@coolgrove.com]

ISBN: 978-1887276-98-6

Library of Congress Control Number: 2022935984

All photographs except those on pages 44, 74,
and 122 are © Clayton Patterson. All rights reserved.

Designed by Laura Lindgren.
Front cover art by John Evans.

This book is distributed to the trade by Ingram Spark.

Coolgrove Press is a member and past recipient of
Community of Literary Magazines and Presses (CLMP)'s
Face Out Re-grant.

Media alchemy by Kiku

coolgrovepress

Contents

Introduction 4

1 · Mickey the Pope 6
2 · Lionel Ziprin Part One 12
3 · Lionel Ziprin Part Two 31
4 · Ned Harrigan 44
5 · The Pyramid Club 52
6 · Boris Lurie and NO!art 56
7 · Linda Twigg 70
8 · The Cradle of Hollywood 74
9 · Father Pat 82
10 · Baba Raul Canizares 94
11 · Jim Power 108
12 · Cochise 112
13 · R. O. Tyler, aka Dr. Uranian 116
14 · Molly Picon 122
15 · LA II 128
16 · Al and Angel Orensanz 132
17 · John Evans 136

Afterword 144

Introduction

Through much of the 19th and 20th centuries, Manhattan below 14th Street was a great cultural brain that dreamed up a fantastic wealth of art and entertainment for the rest of the world. Greenwich Village was one hemisphere, the Lower East Side the other. Across all media and genres, from the loftiest avant-garde to low amusements for the masses, this dream machine changed world culture over and over again.

The Lower East Side and Lower East Siders played key and often dominant roles in everything from blackface minstrelsy to the Broadway musical to drag performance; from vaudeville to television; from Tin Pan Alley to jazz and punk and hip-hop; from the creation of Hollywood to experimental film and video; from Abstract Expressionism and Pop Art to graffiti and tattoo art; and in American poetry, literature, dance, and photography, not to mention cartoons, comics, burlesque, clowning, and the circus. Oh, and prizefighting, and the public library.

Why did so much creativity thrive below 14th Street? The simple answer is: because it was cheap there. Being an artist or a writer or a performer in America is rarely a smart way to earn a living. Creative people flock to cheap places to live and work. Hard as it is to believe now, rents in Greenwich Village were quite cheap from the 19th century into the 20th, and it had the added benefit of being "charming" and leafy and low-density. The Lower East Side didn't possess an abundance of charm, but it was stuffed with very cheap places to live and work, so it attracted its own creative types. The example everyone likes to cite is the fifth-floor walkup at 56 Ludlow Street, where John Cale and Lou Reed formed the Velvet Underground in 1965. The rent was $25 a month.

Besides people in the arts, downtown Manhattan's cheap living attracted other sorts of misfits, rebels, and refugees from the straight and normal life. Both neighborhoods housed more than their share of drug addicts; the less you have to pay in rent, the more you've got for dope. Heroin was a scourge in Greenwich Village well before heroin chic was a hallmark of the East Village. It was on the Lower East Side that Mickey the Pope pioneered his Amazon-like pot delivery service.

The Village had its bohemians and Beats, the Lower East Side its squatters and punks. Gays and lesbians, intellectuals, political radicals, visionaries, and life's pains-in-the-ass also shared the neighborhoods.

As we all know, the era of cheap living below 14th Street is over. The Village succumbed first. The Lower East Side hung on longer, but its transformation in the 21st century has been astounding to anyone old enough to remember what it was like in the 1970s, 1980s, or even 1990s. Cale's $25-a-month walkup would cost at least 100 times that now. The creative people, the radicals and punks and ass-pains, have mostly moved out to cheaper areas in other boroughs.

They left behind a trove of stories. *Offbeats* is a gallery of some great characters from the Lower East Side. A representative handful of visionaries, artists, misfits, and criminals. We could have done many, many more. Think of this as a sampler, like a small box of chocolates.

Clayton has been living in the neighborhood and chronicling its people for forty years. He got John writing about it thirty years ago. Some of these stories we co-wrote, others we wrote individually. We indicate that on the first page of each. A few of them are adapted from articles John wrote in the 1990s for the downtown weekly paper *New York Press*, which he also edited, or more recently for *The Chiseler*. A few are from articles Clayton wrote for *The Villager* and the *Village Sun*. We reproduce them here because the *Press* was a long time ago and poorly archived, and the others have devoted but limited readerships. To us, these are good stories about fascinating characters that should be seen again, and by more people. Like you.

Seventeen chapters from across what could be—should be—multiple volumes of history and stories. It's a start.

. . .

We'd like to thank some people who helped us with this book in various ways: Elsa Rensaa, Ethan Hill, John Szwed, Donna Colelli, Margaret Evans, India Evans, Lincoln Anderson, Donald Kennison, and Daniel Riccuito. Special thanks to Laura Lindgren for the beautiful design and layout.

1 Mickey the Pope

Clayton

Mickey the Pope was the first person to create a major marijuana delivery business in New York City. He turned pot dealing into an industry. He was one of a kind, but he was also typical of a sort of personality drawn to the Lower East Side in those days. A dreamer, obsessed with a vision. A smart businessman who lived and operated in a different reality from other businessmen. A big, tough Jew who didn't give a fuck, not scared of anything, determined and fearless, but sweet and generous to a fault. He lived the life he wanted to live, which was a very Lower East Side attitude.

I had known Mickey for years when I introduced him to the independent journalist Michael Sagar, who wrote a big article about him for *Rolling Stone* in 1991. According to Sagar, Michael "Mickey the Pope" Cesar was born into a well-off Jewish household in Greenwich Village in 1943. His father was an engineer who owned an electronics factory in New Jersey. His mother was the daughter of a very wealthy Englishman who was postmaster general of Jamaica. At some point the family moved to a palatial house in Morris Plains, New Jersey, filled with Chinese vases and other treasures.

So Mickey grew up in a sophisticated environment, but he was always radical and a bit of an anarchist, in the sense that he truly believed we live in an open society and everybody has the right to do what they want. He was very au contraire, and very flamboyant about it. For example, he was gay and didn't give a fuck who knew it, at a time when that was still unusual. Then again, he was a very *big* gay guy, well over six feet tall and as much as three hundred pounds at his heaviest, which I'm sure helped make him fearless. He had a standard greeting, waving his hands in the air and crying out, "Howdy, honey, howdy!" He did that with everybody—friends, strangers, even cops who were arresting him. It was very incongruous, this cliched queen behavior from this huge guy. He would say things like, "I blew every sailor on the *Intrepid*." He also claimed that he liked "young boys," but I never saw him with anyone under eighteen. I think he just said things like that to shock people. He was good at shocking people.

Sagar wrote that Mickey dropped out of high school, joined the navy, and fought with his father, who disinherited him and shoved him in a mental institution. When he got out in the early 1970s he went to Amsterdam. A seaport, it was always full of drugs, prostitution, all sorts of lowlife activities. Mickey fell in with an anarchist crowd who sold pot and hashish. He went into the pot business for himself, and instead of the small amounts the others dealt he went big. He had a giant five-story houseboat on the Amstel River with pounds and pounds of pot on it. He used to say the prime minister of Holland came aboard to buy. He served all the big clubs, and is often recognized as one of the main people who popularized weed "aboveground" in Amsterdam. At some point he declared himself the Pope of Pot, leader of the Church of Realized Fantasies. He created an emblem that was a sickle from the Communist hammer and sickle and a pot plant.

In 1979 he was shot in a lovers' quarrel. Holland extradited him. I believe it was more for being shot in a lovers' quarrel than for the pot. I think pot was probably more accepted in Amsterdam than homosexuality at the time.

He moved to one of the largest, most notorious open-air drug markets in the world. He moved to the Lower East Side. The area was a crime-ridden zone of what many thought of as the joys of life: sex, drugs, and rock & roll. He fit right in. He opened his first business in a storefront on 1st Avenue between 1st and 2nd Streets. It was basically a pot store, customers coming and going all the time, out in the open. He got busted for that in 1981 and spent eight months on Rikers Island. He'd get arrested again in 1983, 1988, 1990.

Given the nature of his business, he had to move his operation around a lot. He'd rent a place, the landlord would catch wind of what he was up to, he'd be evicted and move again. He told Sagar in 1991 that he'd moved his operation at least forty times in the 1980s. After 1st Avenue he moved to Avenue B, between 10th and 11th Streets. This was in the early 80s, when it was still "Alphabet City" and a very dangerous place. Lots of heroin, lots of violence. There were two famous street gangs in the neighborhood at the time. The Allen Boys from Allen Street, who ran heroin on the Lower East Side and in the Bronx and Spanish Harlem, and the Hitmen. Both predominantly Puerto Rican kids, and both very tough. The Hitmen saw all this money and activity on their turf and wanted their protection fee. They confronted Mickey on the sidewalk and demanded protection money.

Mickey being Mickey, he just said, "Fuck you. I'm not giving you nothing, kids."

They shot him five times, on the street. Luckily all they had were .22s, and he was such a big guy they mostly hit fat, no vitals. I remember him laughing later and saying instead of blood coming out it looked like chicken fat. Shot five times and he was still on his feet and conscious when the ambulance arrived. At first the paramedics didn't even believe he'd been hit. Still, it left him with injuries and chronic pains. He came out of the hospital, right back to the block and right back to business. He would hit the boys off occasionally with a bud or two. But never a lot.

I visited him once when he was living on White Street in Chinatown, near the Manhattan Criminal Court. An ABC news team came up to see him—not to shoot a report, but to buy pot. Judges bought from him, lawyers, corrections officers, police. The truth that Mickey understood was that smoking pot was as widespread as it was illegal, through all walks of life. I think that's why he invented his pot delivery system. People who didn't want to be known to buy pot could do it more discreetly. So he started his first call-in delivery services, 777-CASH and DIAL-A-JOINT.

Mickey's pot delivery system was simple but ingenious. He had a bank of five or six telephones and operators. It looked like a bookie joint. Customers called and placed their orders. Not big buys, typically just an eighth of an ounce in an envelope, for $50. The delivery was not made to the customer's address. Instead, a conversation like this took place:

"Where are you?"

"In the Village."

"Okay, be at the corner of 6th Avenue and West 10th Street in thirty minutes."

Thirty minutes later, ten people are lined up on that corner. Meanwhile at the warehouse, one of Mickey's bike messengers—he usually had a fleet of around ten, I think—has loaded a backpack or messenger bag with ten envelopes and ridden off to that spot. The messenger pulls up, takes the cash, hands out the envelopes, and everyone disperses, boom boom boom. Cops aren't watching the spot because it wasn't planned—it was an arbitrary decision made a half hour earlier—and won't be repeated. No fixed location, no consistency, no way for the cops to know where to be to make a bust. Brilliant.

Mickey's messengers never made deliveries after dark. Too many bad characters on the streets at night.

Working for Mickey was a perfect situation for the Lower East Side's squatter kids. They were paid in cash, no records, no taxes. Got up when you wanted to, rolled over to Mickey's. Eat a sandwich there, go out on your bike and make ten deliveries, you've earned a few hundred bucks that day, which goes a long way if you're a squatter. You've got your beer money, some pot, you and your girlfriend are happy.

That lifestyle was an essential element of the neighborhood at the time. In a lot of ways, squatter culture was to New York City what surfer culture was to the West Coast. It was grungier, but a very similar lifestyle, free-living, freewheeling, outside the daily work grind of the mainstream.

At the peak of his business Mickey was said to be bringing in upwards of $10 million a year. He plowed most of it back into the business, buying more pot, expanding his market, going for volume sales rather than quick profits. You never saw him spend it on himself. His ambition wasn't to be rich. It was to get pot out to anybody who wanted it. "Pot is good for you, dear," he used to say. "It's a plant that can save the world." It was the sacrament of his Church of Realized Fantasies. He was in no way the cliched drug dealer with the gold chains and Rolls-Royce. He certainly could have bought those things, but they were of no interest to him. Despite his flamboyant character, his lifestyle was really common. He didn't have a car, let alone a Rolls, and I don't think he even took a cab very often. He walked around town.

And he was extremely generous. He'd say, "Money is like manure, toots, it's meant to be spread around." He was a Fagin-like character, with a whole crew of young men (*not* boys) he looked after. He wanted to offer the people who worked for him health care, but that never happened. I remember a woman with AIDS he took care of, and he gave away pot to other AIDS patients to ease their suffering. He supported many local artists. A lot of creative people from the neighborhood would just come hang out at his place, because they could smoke pot there. This was at a time when buying and smoking pot could still be pretty shaky. Mickey liked having people around. He fed everybody who worked or came by his place. Nothing fancy, there were just always platters of sandwiches and such laid out. He also had a refrigerator packed with raw meat, like raw liver, which he ate. I don't know if that was a dietary choice, a "carnivore diet" thing, or if he did it just to shock people. Probably the latter.

One of his last places was a former comic book store on the corner of Hudson and West 13th Street in the Meatpacking District. The BDSM place Hellfire Club was in the basement below him. He was living and dealing out of there when he did one of his most flamboyant things ever. He went on Howard Stern's radio show and promoted his latest number, 1-800-WANT-POT. Mickey had done media before. He'd smoked pot with Coca Crystal on her cable access show. But that was cable. Howard was just about the biggest voice in talk radio. "He ought to change his number to 1-800-ARREST-ME," Howard snickered.

Why did Mickey do that? He wasn't stupid. Maybe it was that his vision was bigger than his common sense. It was as though he was challenging the cops to come bust him. He pushed it in their faces so hard that they had to deal with it. So they did, raiding the store, arresting him and five of his people, impounding seven pounds of pot. It made the cover of the *New York Post* and a lot of other local news.

By the early 1990s things were unraveling for him. He was living in a tenement on West 43rd Street and 8th Avenue, near Show World. He was pretty sick with cancer, so Elsa and I let him come live with us. We loved Mickey. We made him a Pope of Pot cap, tall like a pope's mitre. Elsa embroidered a pot plant on it. You know how you often name pets after people you like? When we got a cat we named him Mickey.

In 1994 New Jersey prosecutors were desperate to have him extradited to stand trial for a bust there. The New York judge in the case was Leslie Crocker Snyder. She was known as a very, very tough cookie. The Mafia hated her for the brutal sentences she gave them. At times she needed police escorts. But Mickey charmed her like he did so many other people, and she knew he was in and out of the hospital with the cancer, so she prevented his extradition. That was a thing about Mickey. The cops liked him, he got along all right in jail, even one of the toughest judges in the city was fond of him. He had charisma.

He died in February 1995. He was only 52. Pot is now legal in New York, and all sorts of businesses are springing up around it. But let's not forget the pioneers like Mickey, who did it his own way when it was still a radical thing to do. And let's acknowledge that the delivery business Mickey invented was a forerunner of Amazon and Domino's and so many others. How people shopped for pot in Mickey's day is how we shop for almost everything today. He could have been a billionaire corporate CEO if he'd stayed within the lines. But that's not who he was. He was a creative visionary. His goal wasn't pushing product on customers. He just wanted to make people happy. You can get arrested for that in this world.

2 Lionel Ziprin Part One

Clayton and John

Lionel Ziprin was an essential Lower East Side figure, a sage who seemed to walk between worlds, in whom the Orthodox and the avant-garde met, and penniless hipsters consorted with high society. He was never "famous," yet it's remarkable who knew him and came into his orbit.

Clayton met Lionel in the 1980s, at a gallery showing work by the artist Bruce Conner, an old friend of Lionel's. A small man with luminous eyes set in snow-white beard and hair (even though he was only around 60 at the time), Lionel radiated a kind of mystical magnetism that attracted Clayton the way it did many others.

Clayton introduced John to Lionel in the mid-90s. John wrote two articles about him that appeared in *NYPress* in 1996 and 1997. This is the first one.

. . .

The Angel & R. J. Reynolds

In 1951, on the Lower East Side, Rabbi Naftali Zvi Margolies Abulafia published the first American edition of an old Hebrew mystical text, a highly revered but little-read book of the Kabbalah, *The Book of the Angel Radzievsky* (in Hebrew, *Sefer Raziel Ha-Malakh*). It claims to be no less than the first book, ever, in the history of the world.

It says that when God threw Adam out of Paradise, Adam was so terrified and unprepared to deal with the real world that God had to send the angel Raziel to help him out. Raziel gave Adam this book, filled with magical rites, incantations, and the names of thousands of angels Adam and his descendants could invoke for assistance. The book then made its way down through the generations to Noah, who learned how to build the ark from it, and to Solomon, who read in it how to defeat demons.

"Our religious authorities tell us," Rabbi Abulafia wrote in his codicil, "that by keeping this holy book in the home—even though one cannot conceive its contents—it is a safeguard against all evils and misfortunes." And in mystically inclined, devoutly Orthodox households to this day, copies are kept less as reading material than as a protective talisman.

The first known edition of the Hebrew text didn't appear until 1701, in Amsterdam. Exactly 250 years later, Rabbi Abulafia published his private, very limited edition. Some 40 years after that, three remarkable men converged around the idea of publishing the first-ever English translation.

One was Rabbi Abulafia's grandson, the poet and visionary Lionel Ziprin. Another was artist and esotericist Aymon de Roussy de Sales, who happens to be descended from a long line of French nobles, including a saint.

The third was R. J. Reynolds III, scion of the Reynolds Tobacco Co. family. The North Carolina multimillionaire, known as "Josh" to his friends, had a long history of quietly funding research in the occult, esoterica, and fringe sciences.

In their younger days, 1950s–70s, they'd all been variously involved in Beat-era mysticism, hippie psychedelic adventures, and speed-freaking East Village art scenes. Their orbits reached from Tim Leary to Uri Geller to Somerset Maugham, from Avenue D to the Upper East Side to Teotihuacán.

The Book of Raziel might have been the crowning achievement of their silver years. Recent English translations of other kabbalistic texts, like *The Book of Zohar*, had earned great scholarly prestige, not to mention decent academic sales. The three men hoped no less for their translation of *Raziel*, which they commissioned an NYU graduate student to carry out.

Unfortunately, Reynolds died before the translation was finished, and the survivors have bitterly fallen out over it. Ziprin suspects de Sales and/or the translator Joel Hecker of trying to steal the project from him. He and Hecker have registered conflicting copyrights of the work. Both sides have seen lawyers. This version of *The Book of Raziel* could appear in court before it ever appears in print.

It may be that no English translation of *Raziel* had ever been done before because in deep-dish kabbalistic circles it's argued that any attempt to translate it from the Hebrew may be sacrilege and, in effect, cursed. In those old-fashioned homes where it's kept, one of the evils it protects against is theft.

For success, perfect blessing, gratitude, praise—in truth (one will receive) a good portion of all of these if he uses this book with discretion . . . (If one) does and guards everything that is written in it, he will live and be successful in all his actions. This very book can perform all that a person wants.

. . .

Back in the day, Timothy Leary's nickname for Lionel Ziprin was "Rabbi." Now 72 and living in an apartment on East Broadway within a few blocks of where he was born, Ziprin still looks the part—if you picture a rabbi with an elfin sense of humor, angelic visions, and a wild past.

A small, white-bearded man with limpid calf's eyes in a soft pink face, he likes to affect the frock-coated, all-black look. He pushes his longish white hair up under black hats of various styles, from the classic Orthodox style to wide-brimmed Amish hats (shipped to him from Pennsylvania Dutch country) to the occasional baseball cap. He keeps kosher and a strict Sabbath and observes arcane mystical dates on some kind of super-Orthodox calendar that most outsiders, including the handful of Reform or secular Jews I polled, have never heard of. Six days a week he "hangs out" at a crumbling nearby yeshiva, doing little chores for a small group of real rabbis, Holocaust survivors mostly in their 90s, bused over every day from Brooklyn, many of whom have never learned English. ("Days go by, I don't know what they're saying," he laughs.) He believes that angels, demons, and other spirits manifest themselves in the world. He sees and hears them.

I spend several afternoons in his small apartment, crowded with a few big old sticks of furniture, stacks of papers, and those spirits. He and his 18-year-old cat pace around in there with similar nervous energy. He chain-smokes Tareyton 100s. He speaks in the accent and cadences of the Lowest East Side, a kind of verbal Jewish jazz, Yiddish scat, Hebrew hip-hop. Several times when I get up to leave he presses gifts on me. They seem random, but I wonder if they have magical or talismanic intent. One time, from the pages of a book on the Kabbalah, fall two small sheets of gold leaf. I give those back, wondering if it was a test. Other times, he makes me take a web belt and a white lab coat, which I keep. I find two lumps of sugar in a pocket of the coat.

He was born in 1924 on East Broadway and raised by his grandparents after his parents broke up. Abulafia is a Turkish name; in my reading I find a famous medieval Kabbalah scholar named Abulafia. His grandfather "spoke Arabic. He was born in Safed, the mystical kabbalistic city in Galilee, in the north. Where he lies buried now. I brought his body there.

My mother, his daughter, was born there too. When she passed away some years ago I brought her body there to lie by her parents. She came here as a young girl, before World War I."

Growing up in the rabbi's household, "until I was 18 I thought I was living in the Bible. . . . I'd look out and see cars and that would jar me, 'cause I didn't remember any cars in the Bible," he laughs. He once saw some guys on the street wearing black leather jackets and rushed home to tell his grandmother he'd seen "Philistines."

It was in this milieu that Rabbi Abulafia edited and published his edition of *Raziel*, "not to be sold, only to be given to what he felt were worthy people," Ziprin explains. Accordingly, it didn't occur to him to have it copyrighted. He did, however, send a copy to Harry Truman's White House in 1951, suggesting that copies be made to distribute to all U.S. servicemen for their protection. (The country was in the midst of the Korean War.) He got a nice reply on White House stationery, saying his suggestion was being passed on to the Defense Department.

As a boy, Ziprin was sent to a doctor to have his tonsils removed.

"I don't know who distracted the doctor . . . [but] he gave me an OD of oxygen. They didn't think I'd come out alive. I didn't have food or anything. I came out of it 10 days later. And I shook like this—" He holds his hands out in claws and shakes them in palsied quivers. "—till 18 or 19, when I was somewhat cured."

At first they diagnosed it as Saint Vitus' dance, or Sydenham's chorea. "It's a form of epilepsy. Also, I came out with the main child killer in those days, rheumatic fever, which gives you hallucinations even if you don't have epilepsy . . . I couldn't make a bow in my shoe. I didn't know what people were talking about. I had to leave school . . . It was like everybody was on a [movie] screen. Everything was funny. It didn't seem real. They'd be talking there like Bugs Bunny. I didn't know what they were saying . . .

"I began seeing strange things. Lie down on the bed, suddenly I see the planets hundreds of miles down, the whole galaxy. I'm seeing biblical things. This is from the rheumatic fever, with the epilepsy compounded." He remembers "seeing demons and things from those realms. And that stayed with me my whole life."

One day at the hospital where they were seeing him for his rheumatic heart, "All of a sudden this beautiful woman appears, a doctor." He giggles. "This lady, ooo! I'm a kid, I'm alone. I don't need my mother to take me to the hospital. So I'm always standing next to her. I just liked her . . .

And she sees I'm standing next to her, and she gets my chart. This is in the cardiac clinic. You know, I had the epilepsy, I'm shaking, nosebleeds from the rheumatic fever, muscle pains. Oh man, I was a basket case."

She told him to come to her private office. "A butler opens the door, a liveried butler. It was the East 80s, by the river. This office—sumptuous, unbelievable . . . They just give me a shot. A shot, that's it. And every few weeks they give me a little present, like a tie, for showing up."

She turned out to be Dr. Valentina Wasson, who with her husband, formidable New York banker R. Gordon Wasson, would do groundbreaking research on hallucinogenic drugs like peyote in the 1950s. Gordon Wasson's article in a 1957 issue of *Life* was probably the first serious discussion of psychedelics in a mainstream American periodical—and appeared in no small part because the high-society couple were friends with Henry and Clare Boothe Luce, who owned the magazine.

Four years of those shots cleared up Ziprin's shakes, though "I still jiggle in my sleep. I take Dilantin. There was no epilepsy medication then. Now there's a lot. There's a national association for epileptics. We're protected. We carry cards. I think Saint Paul, Saul of Tarsus, was epileptic. It's a really strange disease."

What Wasson couldn't cure were the visions, the hallucinations, the lasting side effects of the epilepsy. "There's some sort of electrical dysfunction I have, a serious dysfunction," he tells me. "You know, I take this medication. Otherwise, if I'm on the street, the police are picking me up. I am doing strange things, I have to hide, I'll die if they put me in handcuffs. I don't hurt anybody. I'm hiding under trees. I'm trying to get home. And when I get home, I lock myself in [the bedroom]. I lose all muscular control. I'm flying. I'm bleeding because I'm like thrust against the walls. Those convulsions can last two days. I'm in such electrical pain that you cannot believe it. It's like you're in the electric chair two days . . ."

Still, Ziprin did venture early out of his grandparents' house. "My mother told me not to cross Delancey Street until I was 21. I'm 17. I hire a horse and wagon on Henry Street five dollars a day for a horse and wagon and two dollars for a bag full of oats, five pounds that would last them the whole day, and I take my things—what things did I have?—from my grandfather's house, and I find a room on 17th Street and 3rd Avenue next to a little Greek church."

Another boarder in the house was "this young girl, early 20s, from Chicago," he recalls. "She says, 'I've been called here by NBC. I'm a puppeteer. They want me to do a puppet show on television.'" This was 1941, the very earliest days of commercial tv broadcast. "There was nothing on television. The first thing on television, sponsored by Firestone Tires, was Milton Berle." Lionel agreed to script a show for her. He called it *Kabbalah the Kook* (pronounced like *cook*).

"So the second program on national television is *Kabbalah the Kook!*" he crows. "I swear to God . . . Coca-Cola and General Foods co-sponsored the show!" He remembers writing 13 scripts, and "I didn't make a dime."

"Since I had lived all those years in the Bible, the other side of Delancey Street knocked me out. I couldn't believe the world. I got destroyed . . . I couldn't make it. I could not make it. I was still having hallucinations, despite everything."

He tried working at "different things. Couldn't stay long on jobs. I didn't know why people fired me, 'cause I didn't know I was sick, you see. Took jobs as waiters, nothing would last." His father, a journalist, got him a job during the war operating a mimeograph machine at a wire service. "I was amazed I could work a mimeograph machine. From there I went to Overseas News . . . I was writing film reviews. From there I became—oh, my father couldn't believe I rose so much, his psychotic son!—I became assistant Middle East editor."

In 1950 he met and married the love of his life, the artist Joanne Eash ("fire" in Hebrew). The very next morning after they were married, the artist and filmmaker Harry Smith showed up at their door unannounced and promptly moved into their lives. The three of them had a complex relationship through the '50s and well into the '60s. Ziprin and Smith fed each other's deep interests in the occult, the Kabbalah, general esoterica. Smith, who was also a folkways anthropologist, would visit Rabbi Abulafia and make field recordings of him singing ancient mystical songs from Galilee.

Joanne and Smith, meanwhile, bonded as visual artists. They would collaborate on a number of grandiose, brilliant—and ultimately doomed—art projects, ranging from elaborately die-cut greeting cards to Smith's extraordinary, hallucinatory animated films. They attracted armies of artists and lots of funding, but somehow the work was never completed or not completed on time, and only fragments—tantalizing, genius fragments—survive today.

They were artists and beatniks, Ziprin says, not businesspeople. They spent too many nights at Birdland, ate too much speed and peyote, did too much heroin. Some died, some went crazy, others moved on. Small wonder, really, that so little's left to show for it.

The Ziprins' home in the 1960s, on E. 7th Street. between Avenues C and D, is now legendary as one of the loci of New York Beat and early hippie culture. A younger friend recently told him it was like an East Village shrine. "I said, 'A *shrine*? It's a miracle I got outta there alive.'" Poets, painters, musicians, drug dealers, sorcerers and magi, Leary and Ginsberg, visiting Arab princes on the hipster tip, groupies, wannabes—and the hordes of undercover agents that type of scene inevitably attracts—all passed through.

"It was a big scene . . . The *whooole* thing was in my pad. I didn't have any control. They took the doors off, they were sleeping in the hall. There were hundreds of people. I didn't know who they were. They were all hungry. It went on. The police wouldn't even touch anyone. There were spirits, right? . . . People were dying every week. People came from all over the world. De Gaulle sent his secretary, bankers . . . the people who started light shows, the rock groups and musicians, and Thelonious [Monk] was coming every night when he was at the Five Spot. I don't know, it was like not a home. I was in terror. I was really in terror. I said, 'This is crazy.'"

When visitors came, making the pilgrimage, "I could sense them already coming down the street . . . My job was to find [them] a room on a spaceship. Then they would come and I'd say, 'This is 7th Street You'll be glad to get off alive. If you wanna place, here it is . . . ' A lot of mysterious things happened. Acid was already on the way. Timothy Leary . . . Those were really weird times. Ha!"

Ziprin doesn't deny he did some drugs in those days. He tried peyote and says he didn't like it. "I wrote a letter to the Agriculture Department in Texas, you send them $5 and they have delivered to your home a bushel of peyote caps. It was legal. Harry said, 'Why don't we try this?'" Of LSD he says, "They were giving it out free. It was in every fridge on every campus in the United States . . . Woodstock, the whole '60s, everybody is dropping acid. I took it a few times. I never liked it. Especially when you would crash . . ."

And there was a lot of speed going down, " 'cause then speed was—you could just get it, there were no laws about it. You could get a pound of crystal meth for $15! Can you imagine?" He took speed himself—prescription amphetamines, he insists, and just to catch up with everybody. "It was like I was in a different dimension than they." On speed, "it didn't seem so macabre, because I was on their wavelength."

To Ziprin, who after all had been seeing spirits and demons all his life, all the crazy, talented, speed-freaking, peyote-tripping people had to be more than mere people. They must be "flesh and blood manifestations" of spirits. "They were hardly in the world," he says. "They were hardly human."

I think it's more than a metaphor for him. He's still living in a biblical world—or maybe a kabbalistic one—where the spiritual plane acts through the physical, working out cosmic struggles of good and evil. Some of the spirits, like the black-leather East Village speed freaks, were dark, earthbound, Nazi demons. "Amphetamine was synthesized by the Germans. That's why the Gestapo could march, and the German armies. They put it in the butter. They didn't even know they were on it. They would march 82 hours. Hitler, I remember listening to him on the crystalphone, 1934, '35, he would talk for 20 hours. He was on speed, they were shooting him up with speed the whole time."

Others—the hippies, the poets, Bob Dylan, the ones who "brought down lightshows so that you could see the planets, three-dimensional, in the room, closer than any space telescope will ever see them in the next 500 years"—they were "aerial spirits, [who] are like hawks, they're like birds, they're like eagles. They live very high. They can take anything but they don't show anything. They are spotless. They can be grown up as Boy Scouts in Evanston, Illinois. You see? The representing spirits, the planetary spirts . . . I could name names, but I won't." And just because they had long hair and dressed like hippies, he notes, "don't think they're like sissies. They are very official . . . They are gentlemen with clean hands."

Ziprin believes that with his electrical disturbances it may be that he's like a faulty radio transmitter, picking up signals from other realms, only his reception's garbled. He's seen the Prophet Ezekiel standing on a street corner, and George Washington communicates with him "not through hallucinations" but through odd coincidences and resonating objects. He swears that if you're around him for very long, you'll see it happening, too.

"If you're out on the street, strange people come to you. My wife would never let me out of her sight . . . Once I was married, I couldn't keep a job, she made me quit the job . . . [She] looked out for me for many years."

He remembers one time his father contacting him out of the blue and asking him to come spend a week with him. He realized that "Joanne must have told him, 'When Lionel goes out, all these strange apparitions appear around him, and all these strange things.' Joanne didn't know whether it was angels or devils or what. In fact, when she left, the night she left, she handed me the Macmillan thick dictionary of angels.

"So I go out with my father . . . We get on the subway and, well, naturally it starts. Three of them come in. One has a cucumber this big." He holds out his hands the size of a watermelon. "Drops it on the floor of the car, and the cucumber starts rolling. And he says—" He giggles, imitating a sinister whisper, "'*You don't know what it is, do you, Mr. Jooonnes?*' Right? And the cucumber starts rolling.

"My father, business suit. Straight, right? Taught semantics at City College. Very straight. Very literary. And the cucumber starts rolling, and one of them makes a dive for it. But I recognize them, see? Because they have like these real shiny eyes."

Do they look like normal people otherwise?

"Yeah. I look at their shoes all the time, 'cause that's a big bad thing to me. I can't tell you what—I see something about the feet, you know? They have these looks. Sometimes they can be rough, like Hells Angels . . . And sometimes they look like what they're called in Tibet, the terrifying deities.' And they *are* terrifying. I mean, you don't want to fool with them, you know? I mean, it's not like a little blonde angel, "'Come go to heaven with me,' like Snow White, with little sparkles." He waves his hand in an aw-phooey gesture, his cigarette trailing eddies of smoke. "Forgedaboudit," he scoffs.

Meanwhile, his father "knows what Joanne told him, that where Lionel goes all this crazy stuff [happens]. So he's sizing it up. He's no fool.

"Let me tell you something, he went with me for a whole week—I just had errands and things to do—at the end of that week, my father aged like 40 years. Nothing happened. They didn't hurt us. They wouldn't talk . . . At the end of the week, that man couldn't walk . . . He *saw*. It was like a heavenly thing. He wanted to see, Joanne put him on this thing to see his son. I can't tell ya, this was a demonstration that was unbelievable."

The last time Aymon de Sales was at Ziprin's apartment—this is recently, after their falling-out—Ziprin watched him turn into a large yellow spider sitting at the kitchen table.

"I see those things just as real," he insists. "If I were an American Indian you wouldn't think anything about it. American Indians, because of their thing, they see totem animals appearing all over. You're gonna tell them it's not so? It *is* so. It is really so. To a white man that's a hallucination. They have been seeing them for thousands of years. I don't know how that works. You just see it."

Joanne left him in 1969—took their four children and moved to California. For a while they lived in Leary's house in Berkeley. She remarried. She passed away in November 1994; Harry Smith had died in November 1991.

"They were very alike people. I think he knew her from a former time . . ."

. . .

For everyone who holds this book and maintains himself in purity, does not bring impurity upon his flesh, does not approach a woman during her period of impurity, does not contaminate himself with the impurity of a corpse, does not bring impurity upon himself through contact with one who is uncircumcised, sanctifies his flesh in living waters, purifies himself to be like God, does not eat any impure thing, does not touch any impure thing, and performs in holiness everything that is written in it (the book), then he meet with success.

One day in 1969, Aymon de Roussy de Sales escorted R. J. "Josh" Reynolds III to Ziprin's apartment at 125 Avenue D, where he'd moved after Joanne left. When I tell Ziprin I'm finding the image of a millionaire tobacco heir from North Carolina wandering Alphabet City kind of curious, he laughs.

"Yeah, I was worried, because we were over a Black Panther key club down below, a bar. Luxy's Bar. It was sorta ethnic," he grins.

"I'm technically an aristocrat," de Sales tells me, "but I was born here."

De Sales is a painter—there was a small show of his Mayan-influenced art in the Village restaurant MaryAnn's—and a writer of psychedelic fables like *The Brown Moo Bird*, which was a book, then a website, then a performance collaboration with Taylor Mead and Larry Rivers. He inherited the title of count from his French father, but he's a casual, frayed-cuff, distinctly American sort of count. At 62, he seems Ziprin's opposite in many ways. Calm, easygoing, a charmer, from high society. He readily admits to a ne'er-do-well, rakehell youth.

In France, the de Saleses have been nobility since the Middle Ages. In the 16th century, Saint Francis de Sales joined the priesthood, did "missionary" work persuading Calvinists to return to the Church, and after a rather comfortable and quiet life died in 1622, at age 55. He is the patron saint of writers and the deaf and is known as "the gentleman saint." Summers, Aymon de Sales flies over and plays the American cousin, visiting the family church and ancestral chateau in Annecy, in eastern France, where Saint Francis is enshrined.

His father was a journalist who came over "to cover the Lindbergh kidnapping" and never went back. He married an American of French descent, and Aymon was born in New York City in 1934. His father died here during the war.

He grew up "in fairly high society." His mother was the editor of *Elle*. They had a duplex penthouse in the East 70s off Park Avenue He was educated at Choate, remembers French toffs mixing with Broadway types at his mom's parties, Carol Channing singing at the piano.

As a boy, he says, "I was always very shy about my family. I remember as a kid saying I wish I was named Smith. I'd get in fistfights with other boys because of my name. So to me it was somewhat of a drag." At best, he grins, the "count" title impressed a few debutantes and "got me into some good parties . . . It wasn't until later when I grew up that I realized that I should be very proud of it."

When he was 17 or 18, he says, his mother's money ran out; he returned to New York to find her "living in this very poor hotel off Broadway. It was such a shock. I really went kind of nuts and sort of became a 'bad boy.'"

It was, he says, the beginning of his rebellious period. He tells me that he went to the Bahamas, where "I ended up living in this whorehouse called Prudence's, a black whorehouse in Nassau," and working as a waiter in a hotel owned by the mother of an old school chum from Choate. "I went to this party, a very smart party, and I'm 22, and I was introduced to this woman, Lady Kenmare, and her daughter. She really wanted to meet me because she'd heard about me living in this whorehouse and she wanted to hear all the stories about her friends—which whores they were meeting with, which ones wanted to be walked on, whatever. So I regaled her with various stories, you know, Lord This did this."

Eventually he married her daughter, and claimed that "I didn't realize at that point that she was one of the wealthiest women in the world." For the next few years he lived the high life with her in Cap Ferrat in the south of France, where he took up painting. "They owned the whole town. Little town. I met Somerset Maugham, a lot of very famous people like that . . . I met Onassis."

"Wow," I say.

"No, the thing of it is, it was not 'Wow,'" he counters. "These are the most terrible people, most of them. Ah, God, they have tons of hangers-on. It's not exciting. You live in this kind of cage, a self-imposed cage . . . I was very young, and I just felt that I was living this non-experienced life. So I left. We never had any children, so." (He would remarry; he lives today in a brownstone in the West 20s with his wife and their five-year-old daughter.)

A few years later, he says, he became part of an odd international gold-smuggling ring that used innocent-looking preppie types like him as the mules. They'd buy the gold in Zurich, sew it into their vests and blue blazers, and fly it to Bombay, where "you could sell it for seven times or ten times the amount" you'd paid for it. "Nobody in that time was going to India from the West, except very old ladies or men on their retirement plans," he smiles. "So when I was in Bombay, if I saw some guy who was in his 20s, I knew for sure what he was, you know? I could spot a fellow gold smuggler a block away. It was kind of an inside joke, this secret smuggler operation where we stuck out like a sore thumb."

Later still, when Leary's people had the idea of cranking out 100 million tabs of acid and turning on all of America, part of the plan was that de Sales would apply his gold-smuggling expertise to smuggling all that acid around.

De Sales first met Josh Reynolds in the late '50s, in the uptown bar Michael's II. Reynolds, a big guy in beat-up motorcycle gear, introduced himself simply as Josh; it was only later, de Sales says, that he found out who the guy was.

Josh Reynolds's grandfather R. J. Reynolds Sr. had founded and built the family's tobacco business in the late 1800s. When he died, Reynolds Sr. left a huge fortune to Reynolds Jr. ("Dick"), who sat on the board of the firm but was not involved in the day-to-day management. His son Josh would have no involvement in the business at all.

Dick Reynolds was a world-class, world-famous playboy and adventurer in the 1930s and '40s, four times married, a huge drinker and constant smoker, a combination that finally killed him in 1964. He was for a time treasurer of the Democratic National Committee; legend has it he once refused to take a thank-you call from FDR because he was too hungover to come to the phone.

Josh, born in 1933, and three younger brothers were Dick's sons by his first marriage. Dick abandoned them when he divorced their mother, and when he died years later, it turned out he had cut all of his sons out of his will (including two much younger half brothers, one of whom, Patrick, would later shock the family by founding the Foundation for a Smokefree America).

They still inherited millions and mostly seem to have done what they could to live up to their estranged dad's wild reputation. De Sales says the four older ones were "North Carolina hillbillies, more like wild mountain boys" than rich sophisticates. They all had a "mad flair." Josh's brother Zach was a daredevil stunt pilot and biker, with the world's largest private collection of motorcycles and his own "biker gang," the Asphalt Prophets. In the '60s he let his hair grow long and reputedly took major quantities of drugs, from acid to codeine. He died in a small airplane crash in 1979.

Of another brother, Will, de Sales says, "Well, they call him Mountain Man." He lives at Devotion, a retreat Dick Reynolds carved out of the Blue Ridge foothills in North Carolina, where he "shoots off his guns, drinks corn liquor, the whole trip."

In an article for the new-age journal *Borderlands* in 1994, de Sales described a psychedelic trip to the Toltec Pyramid of the Sun at Teotihuacán that he, Reynolds, poet Philip Lamantia, and others took on Easter Sunday, 1961.

"Josh was a big, young man with a round, cherub face that was old and young at the same time," he writes. "He was given to going out of his head, but without any drugs . . . He always knew it was coming on, because he began to see things, but he couldn't control it. The last time it happened to him he was walking on a New York street and he began to see . . . faint crystals falling. At first they were small, but they got larger and larger, crystal snowflakes out of the sky—red!—until there was a blizzard of them, and he couldn't see anything else. He was turning a corner on 62nd Street and Lexington Ave., making his way through the silent red crystals falling all around him . . . and the next thing he knew, he was waking up in a straitjacket."

Talking to me, he remembers Reynolds as "very intense, very into mysticism, magic, religion . . . Josh was always seeing the miraculous." The rest of the family "thought he was really kooky . . . He was never on their wavelength."

Over the years, Reynolds showed his interest in esoterica in many ways. He built an ashram in New Mexico. He started a little vanity press to publish his own occultism poetry and edge-science texts with titles like *The Physics of Consciousness*.

In 1980, he gave Andrija Puharich a place to stay at Devotion. Puharich had become famous in the '70s as the man who "discovered" Uri Geller and brought him from Israel to the United States so that Geller's psychic powers could be scientifically tested under lab conditions. He and Geller later had a falling-out when Puharich went off the deep end and began claiming that Geller's powers were derived from space aliens.

At Devotion, de Sales says, Puharich carried his passport with him at all times; he was convinced that an interplanetary invasion was going on, and if a UFO was going to scoop him off the grounds someday, he wanted to have his papers on him in case he was dropped back to Earth in another country. According to de Sales, he also gathered some children he believed were the half-breed offspring of secret UFO-human impregnations and he talked Reynolds into putting a handful of them up at Devotion for a while.

(Amazingly—or maybe just synchronously—Uri Geller came to New York last week as I was writing this. Puharich "was like a mad scientist," he told me. "But brilliant. A genius." They made up toward the end of Puharich's life. "Towards the end he was very sick, he was broke, and it was really very sad . . . Josh Reynolds helped him out.")

De Sales says that when Reynolds and Ziprin met in 1969, "That was a meeting of minds. [Josh] was interested in all sorts of things. Josh had one of those phenomenal minds. They liked each other enormously."

Shortly after, however, "My mother, whose house this is, coming home from work—she was an officer of the New York City Housing Authority—fell," Ziprin tells me. "Had a severe concussion. I didn't want to see her railroaded into a mental institution. So I volunteered. I didn't think it would last *18 years!*"

Moving back to East Broadway, Ziprin effectively removed himself from the world, from the early 1970s well into the '80s. Already a legend of sorts, he became a legendary recluse, writing trunk loads—literally—of poetry, only fragments of which anyone else has ever seen. Even since delivering his mother's remains to Galilee in the late '80s, he's lived very quietly and virtually isolated.

According to de Sales, the early '80s was "the beginning of when Lionel and Josh became very close associates."

Ziprin says they didn't actually see each other that much—he was hiding out here while Reynolds spent much of his time down South or traveling. "In the last 10 years [of Reynolds's life] we corresponded a lot," he explains. "I wrote him at least once a week. Sometimes, when he was ill, toward the end, [I wrote him] every day, for the last six months. We became friends. We wrote a lot. Didn't speak on the phone much. The man was a fabulous mind, many unbelievable interests. Oh, my Lord!"

In 1993, perhaps inevitably, Reynolds got the idea of translating Rabbi Abulafia's book into English. "And he said to me," Ziprin recalls, "'Everything is yours, the copyright, the monies. Just let me get back my investment.' I said, 'Fine.' Aymon, who is a longtime friend, lives in New York, sort of came in, in some sort of supervisory capacity."

"We never, since we entered into this thing, it was never written down," de Sales tells me. "Under those circumstances, while Josh was still alive, I was more or less the go-between, the coordinator. Josh put up the money, it was Lionel's grandfather's book, and I found this guy, Professor [Elliot] Wolfson." It was Wolfson, of NYU's Department of Hebrew and Judaic Studies, who put de Sales in touch with one of his graduate students, Joel Hecker. De Sales hired Hecker to carry out the translation, with relevant scholarly footnotes, at a fixed $45 per page. Wolfson agreed to write an introduction.

In the end, Hecker's translation would run approximately 400 pages, making it a roughly $18,000 project. Maybe nothing to a millionaire, but a lot to be riding on what amounted to a handshake deal.

"It seemed like the only possible way to go with the book," de Sales says. "I mean the only way to go to satisfy Lionel," who, he says, wanted to a book "which would do justice to his grandfather."

But from the instant he met Hecker, Ziprin was most definitely *not* satisfied. In Kabbalah studies, there were two major traditions—a New World and an Old World, let's call them—and they are often in conflict. The newer tradition is the academic one, which studies the Kabbalah as an interesting body of occult literature that has its origins in 12th-century France. To the Old World tradition, all that historical business is fine as far as scholarship goes, but it must rest on a larger, spiritual foundation. These are sacred texts; they derive from God himself and they're not just some interesting branch of literature, but, as Ziprin puts it, a lens through which users of appropriate wisdom and knowledge can interpret biblical texts.

The historic center of this more religious-mystical approach happens to be none other than the ancient city of Safed—Ziprin's grandfather's hometown. The first meeting of Hecker the academic—or "the kid with a little laptop computer" (he was in his early 20s), Ziprin spits—and Rabbi Abulafia's dutiful grandson was an immediate disaster. Hecker never visited Ziprin's apartment again. In fact, Ziprin says they've seen each other only once since.

The work, however, progressed, with Reynolds sending incremental payments to de Sales to be passed along to Hecker, as Hecker delivered more and more pages. (The excerpts quoted here are from a few of those pages, given to me by de Sales.) Ziprin, feeling that he'd been pushed to one side, was getting his copies as the work went on, and hating it. It's too dry, too stilted, too academic. "It has no soul!" he cries. "It has no life! It has no poetry!" At best, he sees Hecker's work as a draft that someone else can take and turn into a proper book. He says he tried to discuss this with Hecker, but his calls were never returned.

In the fall of '93, Ziprin apparently expressed to Reynolds his concerns that he was losing control of his grandfather's book. In January '94, Reynolds's wife died. That same month, Reynolds himself went into the hospital. Like his father (and grandfather) before him, he was dying of smoking-related emphysema, at the age of 60.

"Mr. Reynolds, when he became sick suddenly, in January of 1994, before he went into the hospital . . . called me many times," Ziprin recalls. "I was astonished. And he said, 'Don't worry, Lionel, as soon as the translation is finished, we'll have a contract. Everything will be settled . . . Don't worry about anything.'" Ziprin shakes his head and blows a plume of smoke. "The Angel of Death laughed as he said that. Because Mr. Reynolds went into the hospital right afterwards, and never came out. No contract."

What he does have is a handwritten postcard, apparently from Reynolds, dated the previous October, stating that "as long as the Angel doesn't object . . . since its [sic] your grandfather's translation you should have the sole rights." It goes on: "I hope that all the trouble you are having will start to abate as this project proceeds. I have found that being around Angels is like being on a small board when a great ship goes by—there is a lot of turbulence in its wake."

Reynolds died without heirs in June '94. Longtime Reynolds family lawyer Norwood Robinson is executor of his estate. The will, except for a handful of small bequests (reportedly $10,000 to $50,000) to friends and employees, including de Sales, directed that the estate be liquidated to fund a new charitable foundation. It does not mention the *Raziel* project.

(Robinson, meanwhile, began proceedings instantly—and some say ruthlessly—to have the aged Puharich and another couple of fringe scientists removed from Devotion so it could be sold. In January '95, Puharich evidently suffered a heart attack, fell down a flight of stairs, and died. On the fringe-science circuit, there was grumbling that the lawyer had in effect hounded the old man to death.)

Ziprin gladly admits to hounding Robinson, dunning him with requests for something on paper documenting that the rights to and control of the project were his. At some point Hecker evidently stopped delivery of ongoing work on the translation, holding out the last 100 or so pages, claiming (according to a letter signed by Ziprin's pro bono—and now estranged—lawyer) that he was still owed something in excess of $5,000 for work completed. It's unclear how the payments were allowed to fall that far in arrears.

In August '94, meanwhile, Hecker apparently signed, and de Sales apparently witnessed, an affidavit assigning "joint unqualified copyright and joint unqualified copyright application rights" to the trio of de Sales, Reynolds, and Ziprin. Oddly, Reynolds had been two months dead by August '94. Hecker's motivation for signing this document, if it's legitimate, is also not clear.

Ziprin and Hecker met for the second and last time in April '95, at the office of Ziprin's lawyer, when Hecker refused to sign a document relinquishing his rights to the translation. Ziprin was now thoroughly spooked and convinced that Hecker and/or de Sales was/were going to try to "steal" the translation and have it published without his involvement.

When I ask de Sales for his opinion of why Ziprin would think that, he sighs. "Oh, I don't know. He gets very paranoiac. At least this is something I've heard about him from other people. I don't know what happened. He has something that gets set in his head. And he lives by himself . . . I'm trying to say it's not surprising, but it's sad that it took this turn. I could see it taking this turn when I introduced him to Hecker. When he first met Hecker, he instantly didn't like him," he says, shaking his head. He insists that everyone involved in the project, "including Joel Hecker . . . still understands to this day that whatever we manage to get out of this we'll give to Lionel."

Both Ziprin and de Sales say this is not a conflict over big potential sales. They both tell me they're aware that it's a book with a limited scholarly audience. On top of that, Ziprin clearly feels obligated to pass the first $18,000 of whatever the book made back to the Reynolds estate, as he has always agreed he would. De Sales, meanwhile, tells me that as the project coordinator, he feels personally responsible to Hecker for those unpaid wages.

That June, Ziprin took as much of the translation as he had, 248 pages, and applied for a copyright, listing Hecker as "author of work made for hire." In July, according to a search of Copyright Office records in DC, Hecker also registered a more complete (368 pages) version of the same title.

Last May, Ziprin received an agreement signed by Robinson, stating that the Reynolds estate "hereby conveys to Ziprin all its right, title and interest in the Raziel translation and notes." This summer, Ziprin placed public notice in *Publishers Weekly* and *NYPress*, warning potential publishers not to take on the project.

Now, if either side pursues publishing the translation, the dispute will almost certainly go to court for a judgment as to who has the valid claim. Under current copyright law Hecker, as the creator of the translation and footnotes, has one kind of case to make; Ziprin, if his paperwork holds up, has another.

What he doesn't have, as of this writing, is legal counsel. He has dismissed his lawyer for not pursuing his case avidly enough.

"I've never sued anyone in my life," he says. "But I will sue. I will sue."

Hecker is no longer in New York. He now lives in Canada. I reached him by phone at the Reconstructionist Rabbinical College in Philadelphia, where he teaches three days a week. He declined to comment. He has retained a lawyer in DC; she declined to comment as well.

"Mr. Reynolds asked me many times, 'Lionel, what do you think the Angel wants?' I said, 'I don't know.'"

He who is wise will consider these words, he who is prudent will take note of them. For the paths of the Lord are smooth and sinners stumble on them.

3 Lionel Ziprin Part Two

Clayton and John

John's second *NYPress* article about Lionel Ziprin ran about a year after the first one, in October 1997.

. . .

The Rabbi's Basement Tapes

"My grandfather is stirring," Lionel Ziprin says, worried. His grandfather died in 1955. He's buried in Israel. What's making him restless over there? Maybe the sudden fame of his old friend the late Harry Smith.

Smith's landmark *Anthology of American Folk Music*, originally released as six LPs in 1952, was reissued on CD this past August to universal acclaim. Articles everywhere, a whole book (Greil Marcus's *Invisible Republic*) positioning it as the inspiration for Dylan and everything that happens in American pop music after him.

Ziprin's grandfather must be wondering whatever happened to the records *he* made with Harry Smith. No fewer that 15 LPs, and untold hours more on tape, of nothing more than Ziprin's granddad, recorded in his bedroom on the Lower East Side, singing and telling stories.

Lionel's grandfather was an influential rabbi in the neighborhood, Rabbi Naftali Zvi Margolies Abulafia. A handsome, grizzly-bearded bear in his photos, he was born in 1878 in the city of Safed in Galilee (now Tziat, in northern Israel). An Abraham Abulafia was a highly regarded 13th-century kabbalist. Umberto Eco named the computer in *Foucault's Pendulum* Abulafia. It's a Turkish name; the area was under Turkish rule for centuries.

"There was no money is Israel, in Palestine, under the Turks," Ziprin tells me. "A few Jewish families lived in Jerusalem, in Safed, spread around, very devout. There were no Arabs. This is all baloney, what they say. *Nobody* lived there. [I'd ask] 'Well, how'd you live?' 'We pressed grapes, and sometimes a caravan of Arabs would be riding by, they'd buy the wine.' Under the Turks it was all desert . . . They were all starving. There was no food. The place was really impossible. There was no produce. His rabbi died of starvation, in his arms. In his last words he told him, 'Go from here, and start a home for scholars where this kind of thing will not happen.'"

He boarded a boat heading for Perth, Australia, but because of an epidemic in the Middle East everyone got bounced off the boat in Marseilles. "The little money he had was gone. He got to Paris and took a job sewing berets. Learned to ride a bicycle. Couldn't speak a word of French. Yiddish, Hebrew, and Arabic he could speak."

Eventually he made his way to Philadelphia, then the Lower East Side, and brought the family over, except for one son who stayed behind and was killed—kicked by a camel in a Jerusalem street. "There wasn't a day till she died that my grandmother didn't cry that she left him."

Ziprin was born in 1924. His father left his mother when he was very young, so he was raised in his grandparents' house. He never set foot north of Delancey Street as a kid. He likes to say it was like living in the Bible. "They walked barefoot in the house, the whole place was like a tent. They spoke Arabic when they wanted privacy, so I shouldn't understand." They ate with their fingers, like Arabs, "but if guests came, they brought out a spoon and a fork," he giggles.

His grandfather "went to work for Metropolitan Life Insurance. And I'm sure whatever he touched would've succeeded. But he wouldn't work Saturday. They put his name on the door, and his wife said, 'You can't have your name on a door where the office is open Saturday.' So he gave it up. And he got very angry. He said, 'Well, what can I do in America?'"

It was the Depression. "There were no lights in the house. Everybody got these little potbelly stoves, you put a chimney in the wall, and at night we went out scavenging for pieces of wood to put in the stove. Potatoes were five cents for five pounds. That was our main staple . . . I remember going every day to school with no soles on my shoes. I had to tie cardboard. And I said to myself, 'It's good I'm a kid, because if I was an adult and had to walk in the streets with cardboard tied to the bottom I'd really feel bad. But this way, it's just like fun.'

"The Depression lasted until the draft began. You see, that's why nobody did anything about Hitler. Because [when] Hitler came to [power] in '31, '32, '33, everybody knew it. I knew it. I saw the whole thing in a vision happen, in about 1933, just before he was made chancellor, and I was screaming and crying and I ran up the steps—there were all rats in the house, the cats wouldn't even catch any, every house, the slums—and I was screaming, 'Grandmother, help me.' And I said, 'You know what's gonna happen?' Well, nobody could protest [Hitler] because nobody had any food. Everything was, 'Where is the next piece of wood?'"

He remembers the whole family "out scrounging for dollars . . . We were living in such conditions. I was sleeping under the dining room table." His grandfather collected funds for Hebrew charities. His mother—Bathsheba, called Sheba—devoted her life to public housing and "burying the slums." She became a top bureaucrat in the city's public-housing administration in the 1950s and '60s.

Ziprin's grandfather "was a descendant of the family of David. How do you like that? There are three lineages that are Davidov. The Satmar rebbe, the Beyonner rebbe—who was also my rabbi, we lived across the street—and my grandfather. But my grandfather didn't make a big thing of it. He only told me once or twice. He was more proud that his cousins [ancestors of his cousins] fought under Washington. They were Masons. They were captured by the British. The British captain took them on a boat. It turned out the British captain was a Mason, and he releases them."

Rabbi Abulafia was very patriotic. "He was a *Republican*," Ziprin laughs. "The only Republican in the Depression on the Lower East Side! He doesn't believe in the government doing everything. He was a Republican, made my mother become a Republican, joined the Republican Club and didn't speak one work of English. When Israel was taking all the money from the United States, he'd sell bonds. 'You can't go around like a beggar. This is not how the world works. That's why everything is wrong there. Everything is begging, begging, begging.' He was like an old-fashioned American. I didn't meet another Republican on the Lower East Side . . . In the middle of the left-wing, liberal—he didn't want to hear about it."

At the end of the Depression, when "money started dribbling back into the economy," Rabbi Abulafia founded the Home of the Sages of Israel. "He bought the building that was the Jewish Maternity Hospital in East Broadway, which was actually nonsectarian. Everybody got born there, the whole East Side was born there. I got married in that building. I got married *and* born in that building."

The "sages" came from old folks' homes, from the homes of their children in the neighborhood; came from Eastern Europe and the Middle East, and from the concentration camps ("I used to see the tattoos"). "He got rabbis, and only scholars. All these scholars, you could see from their faces. About 40 or 50." They lived upstairs, in converted hospital rooms, and he built a big library down below where they could study the Talmud and kabbalistic texts.

. . .

In 1950, Ziprin married the artist Joanne Eash. The very next morning after they were married, this strange artist-anthropologist-filmmaker-magician Harry Smith showed up at their door unannounced, and promptly moved into their lives. Ziprin and Smith fed each other's interests in the occult, the Kabbalah, general esoterica. Ziprin had an ill-fated greeting card company, Inkweed, that employed Smith for some years. Bathsheba bought many of the cameras and other equipment Smith used to make his avant-garde films. And in fact Ziprin says it was through his grandfather that Smith met Moe Asch of Folkways Records, who put out the now-famous *Anthology* in 1952.

The story of how Smith and Ziprin's grandfather came together involves a long windup and a discussion of the Hebrew liturgical calendar.

"From the second day of Passover, for 49 days, are a most mysterious 49 days," Ziprin explains. "It's called the Omer. An Omer is a measure of barley." Hebrews offered up an omer of barley on the second day of Passover. From that day to the feast of Shavuoth, a harvest feast, is 49 days. "It has to do with the period of cutting the barley. It's a whole ritual with the reaper. In the field it starts, the reaping. That's one level, cultural."

On another, symbolic level, the Jews leave Egypt on Passover night and spend 49 days in the desert. The 50th day, Shavuoth, is the day "when the law is given, the Torah is given."

Traditionally, the Omer is a time of mourning. "These days are fraught, because of the journey. Tremendous difficulties have beset the Jews in those seven weeks, historically." The massacres following the failed rebellion of Rabbi Shimon bar Kochba against Hadrian's imperial Roman army occurred during the Omer. Depredations during the Crusades are remembered during the Omer. "The Inquisition was set, Hitler started his thing, so many things. People write about it, they can have fifty pages of disasters."

Consequently, you're not supposed to begin any new ventures during the Omer. Don't get married, don't start a business, don't even get a haircut. Also no music or other entertainment.

"Now, there's one day that's an exception to this rule. The 33rd day of Omer." Marriage, all of it is permitted that day. "Because on that day, the mouth of everything they call Kabbalah, who passed away two thousand years ago, after being imprisoned with his son, buried up to the neck for thirteen years in a cave escaping the Romans in ancient Palestine—Shimon bar Yochai—died. Whenever they speak of kabbalism, that is the source." Mystical kabbalists believe that the major book of the Kabbalah, the Zohar, documents discourses given by bar Yochai to his son in the cave.

Shimon bar Yochai's death is celebrated on the 33rd day of Omer, Lag B'Omer. "Before he died, since he had this life of thirteen years in the cave, the revelations came, and his son recorded them. He said before he died, 'When I die, people should sing and dance.' That was during the time that you're not supposed to sing and dance. So the way it turned out, on that day, people do marry—they make a point of marrying on that day, because it's supposed to be, like, lucky."

In fact, Lag B'Omer is the occasion of a huge party outside Shimon bar Yochai's cave near the town of Meron, with bonfires and ecstatic whirling dances and song.

"Tens and tens of thousands of people come for the last 2,000 years like pilgrims from all over the world, but mainly Jews from the Arab countries, and dance around his grave all night, and sing. I have never been there. I would sure like to witness it once.

"Now, my grandfather, I thought he was an incarnation of this man. I never told him that. You don't talk to him like that. Forget about it. Every year, he made a party on Clinton Street, there was a place called Clinton Hall where they make bar mitzvahs and wedding parties. He'd make a party and invited all the people in New York that were from like Galilee and that area. He built a brass tree—I don't know where this is—in which candles were lit, and all the names of the saints and ancient rabbis. And they would dance—the women wouldn't, the women would sit—the men would dance. They'd dance on their heels and they'd sing all these songs. My grandfather would wear a fez—I have the fez here—and a white satin robe, and they'd sing and they'd dance all night long, as if they were at the Shimon bar Yochai's grave in Meron."

Because Smith had a vast interest in all kinds of music—he'd done anthropological recordings of American Indian rituals, for example—Ziprin invited him to his grandfather's Lag B'Omer celebration.

"I said, 'Listen, Harry, I'm going with Joanne. You wanna go?' Yes, he would love to do that. I said, 'You gotta wear a yarmulke, it's a religious thing. You wear the hat.' Fine. He looked already like a little rabbi, with the beard, oh God, everybody thought he was Jewish. You know Harry, skinny little Harry, practically blind, right?

"So he came. And the dancing is going on, we're sitting, and Harry says, 'What's the music?' He'd never heard anything like it. And he's recording everything. Hours and hours on tape. That's Harry. He was never without a tape recorder . . . At the end, everybody starts going home. So Harry shows my grandfather the tape. My grandfather looks at me and says, 'What is that?' Harry says, 'Listen.' He plays him a tape. Well, my grandfather's astonished to hear his voice on the tape there. Magic, right? That did it. So Harry says to him—and I'm the interpreter, but they got along somehow—would he like to make some songs and he will tape them.

"Well, that began a two- or three-year session."

At the time, Ziprin's grandparents and mother were living on East Broadway, next door to the Home of the Sages, on the third floor. "My grandfather was very heavy, and when he got old he could not walk up three flights. It was very hard for him. He was light on his feet, but very heavy, always. So he had a room on the ground floor, in the back, facing Division Street." Harry filled that room with recording equipment (which Rabbi Abulafia bought for him) and it became their studio.

"I go into the room, I saw these recording things nailed to the walls, machines. My poor grandfather. He was living now and sleeping in a recording studio. I don't know. My grandfather doesn't speak English and Harry speaks no Yiddish. So how did they get on all those years?" He laughs and shrugs.

"So he's recording with Smith every day. Who knows what kind of conversation went on? My grandfather never said anything, except he said to me in Yiddish once that in another life he thinks Harry was Jewish. Because by then Harry had become a confirmed kabbalist, a scholar, in English, of kabbalism. He was always in the library, taking all these magical manuscripts out, talking to my grandfather, bringing him Hebrew books. Harry collected thousands of Hebrew books. Harry is a madman, a magical madman."

The songs Smith and Rabbi Abulafia committed to tape "are songs that are known everywhere, but with the Jews, the ones from Poland sing one way, from Hungary another way, from Romania another, Russia another. It's like dialects in English. In the South you speak one way, in Maine another way. So these are how he always sung, from where he was raised, ancient."

Ziprin avers that his grandfather "makes Caruso's voice like nothing." What I hear sounds more like an old Plains Indian shaman—on some songs he even beats the monotonous rhythm on what sounds like a tom-tom—combining ritual chants with scenes from *The Threepenny Opera*. These are very, very old, droning songs interlaced with brief Yiddish narration. For a goy, the biggest revelation was hearing Rabbi Abulafia sing the upbeat "Yovo Adir Bimheiro" and realizing that it's note for very note the tune of the ur-classic surf music song "Miserlou," the one they danced to in *Pulp Fiction*. Who knew Dick Dale is Jewish?

Ziprin doesn't know how many hours of singing Smith recorded. Hundreds anyway. He shows me one box filled with a few dozen old reel-to-reel tapes, and there was another, or maybe two more boxes, apparently lost now.

In 1954, "My grandfather said, 'With Harry you could go on taping till the world ended. Something has to be done.'" So with his own money, Rabbi Abulafia had 1,000 copies of a 15-LP set pressed and packaged. Those 15 LPs "take about two weeks to hear!" Ziprin exclaims. "I think the whole thing cost him about 35 grand," which was a lot in those days. One day, numerous crates of records appeared and were shoved into Rabbi Abulafia's room with everything else.

Rabbi Abulafia died in 1955, not long after the records appeared. He was told that the Home had to be moved—the building was to be torn down, ironically, for housing. Even though it was assessed at $600,000 and a nice, new facility would be built for the Home on Bialystoker Street, Ziprin says he was inconsolable about the move. "*This* was my grandfather. Not some newfangled building over there."

. . .

They buried the rabbi in New Jersey, " 'cause he had 11 graves [burial plots] there, which he just bought. And I said, 'He doesn't lie in New Jersey. He has to go to Israel.' They said, 'What are you crazy? How do you know he wanted to go to lie there?' I said, 'What are you asking me how do I know? He was closer to me than to his children.' Just a couple of days before he passed away, someone said to him—my grandfather never went to a movie or to visit a person or anything—some rabbi passed him and said, 'Why don't you go on a vacation?' He said, 'When I go on a vacation I'll go to Israel.' I knew exactly what he meant, 'cause three days later he died. Of course he wanted to go to Israel. His family lies there. He was born there.

"I fought and fought and fought and fought for nine months, until I got them—'Ooo, the expense!' It cost a lot of money. Cost eight or nine thousand dollars. Customs here, health department there, not a simple thing. Nine months later they exhumed his body. They took him to Safed to lie in the ancient cemetery there. It's about 2,000 years old. And I got a letter from the holy brotherhood that buries people—it's not that they're holy, it's that the work they do is sacred. It's no reflection on them. They take care of burials. They told me that when they opened the coffin—because in Israel you don't lie in the coffin, you just wrap the body in the shroud—they described that his body was absolutely like a child, like 'white marble.' His body was fresh, no decomposition.

"So now I am faced with what am I going to do with all these records?" Ziprin recalls. His grandfather had said, "'You distribute it.' He must have known he was going . . . What do I do with all these albums? I am broke. My greeting-card business collapsed for the third time. I'm living in a cold-water studio flat with two or three children. I say to my mother and her brother, 'You gotta give me some money. I gotta get a room, buy steel shelves, put the albums up, and I will investigate how to sell them.' His son says no . . . He puts it this way: 'This is all sacred stuff. I'm not having my father's voice playing in some record-selling store on 14th Street and Union Square.' I said, 'Why are you saying 14th Street? They'll go to universities, to synagogues, to religious groups, ethnic. They record Tibetan music. This is like an important ethnic collection, a major, major collection. There's never been a collection of this sort.'" No go.

For lack of anywhere else to store them, his mother had the crates of records and most of the tapes moved to the basement of a Bronx public-housing project she administrated. There they sat for years, unheard and largely forgotten. By the 1970s Ziprin was a recluse, holed up in his East Broadway apartment looking after Sheba, who was in the process of going mad. Smith, after some huge reversals of his own, had become a drunk, sponging off friends like Allen Ginsberg.

At some point in there, "All of a sudden, word comes that the sprinkler system broke in the basement, and all the records are destroyed." Lionel went out to the Bronx and found "everything is wet, ruined, broken—the fire department smashed everything . . ."

Luckily, his mother had kept the masters for the 15 LPs at home. Ziprin salvaged, he says, a few thousand of the records and two or three big boxes of the tapes. He stored them in the new Home of the Sages on Bialystoker Street.

In 1979, through a well-connected friend, PolyGram/Deutsche Grammophon briefly took an interest in the recordings, but nothing came of it. Sometime later, Ziprin went over to Home of the Sages to check on the stuff, and "All the records are gone. I said, 'Where are the records? Thousands of records?' 'We don't know.'" He mugs a big, vaudevillian shrug. "They still don't know."

Today what's left that he knows about are the 15 masters, the one box of tapes, and two or three pristine sets of the vinyl LPs.

And now, I suggest to him, with Rabbi Abulafia stirring, with Smith suddenly famous. . . .

"Yeah, but in the meantime Harry is starving and drunk all those years!" he cried, cutting me off. "He's going from place to place. He lives at Ginsberg's place. Things are not so great . . . When Harry was drunk I couldn't see him. I *couldn't* see him. I didn't know who he was. I couldn't stand the way he talked. I couldn't see him hardly, except I'd run into him. And now all of a sudden Harry's famous." He starts yelling and waving his cigarette around. "Oh, he had this big effect! The Invisible Republic! Bob Dylan! Why didn't Bob Dylan give him $10? Did Bob Dylan ever give him a dime? *No!* Jerry Garcia gave him 10 grand a year because Allen interfered. Allen was sick of being the sole supporter."

Smith died, broke and broken, in November 1991. "Harry's last words to me, when I saw him last, at a photographic show on 57th Street, when we shook hands after years when we didn't see each other too much, he sang me one of these songs, and he remembered it *perfectly*," Ziprin marvels. "On the street. About a year before he died."

Now here he is, the only one left, with his grandfather's onus still on him. "We still have what we have," he goes on, with another theatrical shrug. "I feel that something maybe can be rescued from all this."

. . .

Postscript

Long as they are, these articles were just snapshots. There was a lot more to Lionel than the befuddled naif he presented in them. The milieu he and Joanne created in the 1960s was a spiritual and creative nerve center of hip America, a node of the underground when there was still an underground and it still exerted an influence on the mainstream. Lionel's magnetic spirit (or spiritual magnetism?) attracted an extraordinary array of people—Harry Smith, Timothy Leary, Josh Reynolds, Clare Boothe Luce, Count Aymon de Roussy de Sales, and more. The '60s were like that; the cream of the underground and high society and the corporate world converged and conversed more than you'd see today. Lionel was an essential connection point for that.

He was an impressive scholar of Judaica, the Kabbalah, the occult, a self-made sage at home at the Home of the Sages. Clayton recognized the little sheets of gold leaf Lionel slipped to John as classic kabbalism. The Kabbalah sage doesn't hold classes in it. There's no "Open your books to page fifty-three." Lessons are oblique and indirect. There was a message in those sheets of gold leaf. It was a hidden message, but it was right there in your pocket. Same with the *Sefer Raziel*. Even if you know how to read it, its meaning is all in codes and symbols.

Lionel had many more strange stories than were captured in the articles. If you heard them from anyone else you'd doubt them, but coming from Lionel you thought, "Well, maybe . . ." There were ones about the U.S. intelligence agents staking out his East 7th Street house to keep tabs on Leary and others who went in and out. The nights he and the artist Barbara Remington, who did the famous cover illustrations for the first paperback edition of *The Lord of the Rings* in 1965, stood out back of that house and watched the skies of New York City for UFOs. There was the mysterious CIA agent—or was he Mossad?—who for a while rented out the middle bedroom of Lionel's apartment. No one ever saw him, except for the watch he left Lionel when he died. And there was the limo that for a while would pick Lionel up downtown and ferry him to Rockefeller Center, where he'd take the elevator up to a luxe boardroom, where he'd consult with Rockefellers and high-level representatives of the government on using mylar, which he and Harry Smith had worked with, to coat the nose cones of ballistic missiles. Coming from Lionel, knowing what one knew about his life, it all sounded wildly improbable yet not totally implausible. Who would have thought the rabbinical poet of the Lower East Side and the Reynolds tobacco scion would become friends and colleagues? Lionel certainly wasn't bragging or trying to puff himself up when he told these tales. If anything, the way he told them was excruciatingly self-effacing.

Lionel's health began to fade in the 2000s. He called John once to tell him about a biopsy where "they went in through my *ass* and found a polyp the size of a *rose*," emphasizing ass and rose in a comically whiny up-tilt that was pure Jewish scat. If anyone had polyps like roses, it would be Lionel.

He died of pulmonary disease in 2009. He was 84. Pretty good for a lifelong chain-smoker. He was buried with his grandfather and other ancestors in Safed.

No English translation of the *Sefer Raziel* was published in his lifetime. A few have appeared since.

Although a few small labels spoke with Lionel about Rabbi Abulafia's recordings, nothing came of it at the time. As of 2021, a new set of the recordings is said to be in the works. This is possibly due to the continuing and growing interest in Harry Smith. Clayton helped Columbia professor and author John Szwed as he researched a new biography of Smith, especially with his research into Lionel and his grandfather.

Lionel often spoke in mysterious ways about a few trunks of items he kept in the apartment. He made them sound like biblical arks containing magical, ancient, powerful talismans. He fretted over what would become of them after he passed on.

When he did, his daughter Zia became the executor of his estate. In *Jews: A People's History of the Lower East Side*, she writes about her fraught relationship with her father. Her mother left Lionel in 1969, driving to Berkeley in a VW bus, taking Zia, who was seven, her sister, and two brothers. Out there they joined Timothy Leary's menagerie. Zia didn't see Lionel again until she came back to New York City when she was 18. Joanne died in 1994.

Zia arranged to have the contents of Lionel's trunks placed in a large old safe in the Brooklyn loft of the artist Carol Bove. Writing in the magazine *Frieze* in 2014, Andy Battaglia described the trove as "books, boxes, manuscripts, tracts, paintings, prints, recordings . . . Some of his belongings are religious documents that date as far back as the 17th century. Others align with postwar American forays into formative psychedelia and realms of the occult. Much of it is esoteric; all of it is mysterious, suggestive or at least a little bit otherworldly and strange."

Among all that was some of Lionel's own poetry. To say that he was prolific would be a supreme understatement, yet he never seemed all that interested in seeing his writing published. A handful of his poems appeared in literary magazines during his lifetime. T. S. Eliot evidently wrote him to praise one of them. Yet another unexpected connection. But mostly he spent years adding line after line to gigantic, epic works like "Sentential Metaphrastic," a "poem in progress" of more than a thousand pages. "I call it the longest and most boring poem since Milton's 'Paradise Lost,'" he told *The Jewish Quarterly*.

In his archives Clayton has some 32 videos he made of Lionel between 1988 and 1991. In 1988 he shot a two-hour video of Lionel reading aloud his *Clues to a Scotland Yard Mystery*. In 1989 he shot a whopping twenty hours of Lionel reading from another of his epic poems, "The Book of Logic." Lionel called it "supposedly an Epistemological Fantasy, a pretensive exposition of Logistica Talmudica," which was "in fact a Slam-Bang Exorcists Ritual which effectively guarantees subsummation of 'All-That-Ails-Thee' and 'Peace-Everlasting' to such precious few as having the stamina to see, hear, and bear it."

Precious few did. They screened the tapes at Anthology Film Archives in 1989, two hours a night, planning a 10-night series. By the third night there were only two friends of Lionel's in the auditorium (Debra Freeman and Ira Cohen, another Lower East Side poet and sage) with Clayton and Lionel. The rest of the series was nixed.

Unsurprisingly, the only Lionel Ziprin book published in his lifetime, *Almost All Lies Are Pocket Size*, is no typical book. It's a wooden box, like a cigar box, that you open to find a little booklet, some loose sheets, a small flexidisc recording of Lionel, and a photo of him. More talismans. It was produced in 1990 in a run of 350 by Sandy Rower and Judy Upjohn's Flockophobic Press, after Clayton introduced them to Lionel. Clayton had met them in Jean Noel Herlin's antiquarian bookstore at 68 Thompson Street, another magnet for creative people. Rower is a grandson of Alexander Calder and father of the composer and curator Gryphon Rue, who has collaborated with Clayton on various projects. Judy is of the pharmaceutical company Upjohns. Still more unpredictable connections.

In 1958, when he was 34, Lionel put together close to 300 poems to celebrate the fifth birthday of his eldest boy, Leigh. It was a family thing, never published in Lionel's lifetime. Philip Smith, a Lionel and Harry Smith scholar (but no relation), found it in the safe with other Lionel papers, and *Songs for Schizoid Siblings* was posthumously published by The Song Cave in 2017. Some of the poems read like slightly off-kilter nursery rhymes:

hickory, dickory duck
the mouse ran out of luck

Others are like nursery rhymes for grown-ups:

when priapus starts to moan
everybody holds his own

And some suggest Lionel was thinking along kabbalistic, tarot, or alchemical lines:

> the lad who rides alone is one
> who'll find the lady on the sun.
> when caught, inside that black balloon,
> he'll place her back upon the moon.

Lionel also apparently did some uncredited writing for Dell comic books, including an early '60s series called *Kona, Monarch of Monster Isle*. Hard to verify, but again, not entirely implausible knowing Lionel.

Although Lionel moved on in 2009, Clayton still feels the connection. In 2020, when his lifelong partner Elsa began to require 24-hour care, Clayton arranged for her to enter the nursing facility of Rabbi Abulafia's Home of the Sages.

4 Ned Harrigan

John

John wrote a version of this for *The Chiseler*.

. . .

>Ireland and Italy,
>Jerusalem and Germany,
>Chinamen and nagurs,
>And a paradise for cats;
>Jumbled up together
>In snow or rainy weather,
>They represent the tenants
>In McNally's row of flats.
>
>The great conglomeration
>Of men from every nation,
>The Tower of Babylonium
>Couldn't equal that
>Peculiar institution,
>Where brogues without dilution
>Were rattled off together
>In McNally's row of flats.
>   —Ned Harrigan, 1882

For most of the 19th and 20th centuries, the Lower East Side was the doorway to America for immigrants from around the world. For its time it was the most diverse urban area in the world (that's said to be Queens now). Mostly poor, some terribly so, people in the neighborhood lived all crammed together in dreadful 19th-century tenements, then in the 20th-century public housing that replaced tenements without always improving on them. They couldn't help but encounter one another's cultures, cooking, languages, religions, ethnicities. They couldn't help but hear each other, smell each other, sometimes sleep with each other, often fight each other. It was the Lower East Side that Israel Zangwill had in mind when he wrote his 1908 play *The Melting Pot*, about people from around the world forging a new American culture.

Many of the firsthand accounts of life in the neighborhood's slums of the 19th century come from tourists like Charles Dickens, muckraking reformers like Jacob Riis, sensationalizing journalists, and middle-class Protestant ladies who ventured there to hand out Bible tracts and reclaim the morals of its heathens and papists. But some of the most intimate and certainly funniest depictions were written by a man who grew up there and went on to be one of the most popular showmen and songwriters of the late 1800s. Along the way, Ned Harrigan helped lay the foundations of the Broadway musical, and even the tv sitcom.

. . .

Ned Harrigan was born in 1844 and raised in a small brick house on Scammel Street, which no longer exists, a couple of blocks below what are now the Manhattan ramps of the Williamsburg Bridge. From Dutch times, that area was known as Corlear's (originally Corlaer's) Hook, for the finger of land that poked out into the East River. Landfill refashioned the hook into more of a hump, and in Harrigan's time it was so Irish it was popularly known as Cork Row. Harrigan's father was a former seaman who worked in the bustling shipyard a few blocks away from their home. As a lad Ned dove from those busy piers and worked in the shipyard himself (plugging holes in ships' hulls with the material called oakum, a word that mutated into the theatrical term for filler, hokum). According to biographer Richard Moody, Harrigan shipped out as a young man, working as a deckhand on a banana boat that sailed from South Street to New Orleans, then kept going, west to San Francisco. He began his stage career there in 1867, singing blackface minstrel songs and doing comic Irish turns in low-rent concert halls known as melodeons, where the entertainers competed with drinking, gambling, and whores for the all-male patrons' attention.

In Chicago he met Anthony Cannon, not yet sixteen, an Irish youth from Worcester, Massachusetts. He was a petite and pretty boy who sang in a sweet falsetto, and had, Harrigan said, the face of an angel on a valentine. He specialized in female impersonation. This was not as outré as it might sound today. A handsome boy playing a pretty girl was a familiar device, especially in comedies and farces. Cannon reputedly excelled at it to the point of fooling many an audience.

As they teamed up, Cannon took a new stage name, Tony Hart, which flowed better with Harrigan. Harrigan also teamed with bandleader and songwriter Dave Braham, who'd become his father-in-law. Harrigan wrote short, comical sketches and song lyrics, Braham wrote catchy tunes, and Hart played and sang both male and female roles. They worked variety theaters, the precursors to vaudeville, where they shared crowded bills with blackface minstrel troupes, acrobats, jugglers, magicians, trained bird and dog acts.

Harrigan & Hart quickly rose to the top of the bill and found a permanent home on Broadway at the Theatre Comique. The Broadway theater district was not then around Forty-Second Street, which was still the uptown outskirts, but downtown, where all the people were. The Theatre Comique was at 514 Broadway, below Spring Street.

In 1873 Harrigan & Hart hit paydirt with a ten-minute sketch and signature song, "The Mulligan Guard." Like all of Harrigan's best work it was a farcical comment on current affairs happening right outside on the streets of the city. In the mid-1800s it was all the rage for patriotic American males to join gaudily uniformed militia units. As military organizations they were largely useless, trained only to march in parades, not to fight or shoot, as they demonstrated with their often dismal battlefield performances in the Civil War. In truth they functioned more as social and drinking clubs. Immigrants found themselves banned from these organizations, so they formed their own German, Irish, Italian, Scots, and French volunteer militia. Factories, shipyards, shops, and every fire company had one. Determined to prove their superiority to the nativists' militia by actually learning how to shoot their rifles with accuracy, they were called target companies. Their interest in riflery and marksmanship helped to inspire the founding of the National Rifle Association in New York City in 1871.

In Harrigan's sketch, the Mulligan Guard consisted only of Dan Mulligan, played by Harrigan in a crooked fez and with giant epaulets, and the petite Hart as Captain Hussey, in a ridiculously tall shako with a long sword dragging on the ground. The sketch, all slapstick tomfoolery, was an instant hit with audiences, the talk of Broadway. The song itself traveled around the world as sheet music and became one of the most widely known and played band tunes of its day. British troops in India march to it in Kipling's *Kim*. For Harrigan's many fans who couldn't read sheet music, his lyrics were disseminated in humorously illustrated booklets called songsters.

> We shoulder'd guns, and march'd and march'd away,
> From Baxter Street we march'd to Avenue A,
> With drums and fife how sweetly they did play,
> We march'd march'd march'd in the Mulligan Guard.

Knowing a good thing when he'd written it, Harrigan developed the Mulligan sketch into a series of full-length farces—*The Mulligan Picnic, The Mulligan Guards' Ball, The Mulligan Guards' Surprise*, and so on—that made Harrigan & Hart the comic kings of Broadway from the mid-1870s to the mid-1880s. Harrigan called his formula "slambang, melee, and grand melee," which basically meant ascending orders of slapstick chaos, a typical comedy formula at the time. In the grand climax of one play, for instance, the Mulligan Guard are feasting on one floor, the all-black Skidmore Guard above, when the second floor caves in and the Skidmores drop onto the Mulligans' heads. The Theatre Comique's packed houses evidently found it hilarious. Harrigan was innovating what would become the American musical. And because the Mulligan series followed the lives and misadventures of a core of familiar and well-loved characters from one theatrical season to the next, he was also inventing what we know as the sitcom; the Mulligans and their neighbors are in many ways precursors of the Kramdens and Nortons, their Knights of the Mystic Star a forerunner of the Raccoon Lodge.

By the early 1880s they were packing them in at their own Harrigan & Hart's Theatre Comique at Broadway and Waverly Place, a block west of where the Public Theater is today, with their own orchestra, led by Braham, and their own troupe of performers. Harrigan wrote, produced, directed, and performed. One explanation for their enormous success is that Harrigan was writing from life. Superficially his characters were not unlike the broad racial and ethnic stereotypes that were the meat and potatoes of American popular theater and fiction at the time. Although blackface is the best known and most controversial, many other stereotypes strode and capered across the stages and pages of the time: drunken, brawling Irishmen; thickheaded Germans, called "Dutch" from the same Americanized approximation of *Deutsch* that yielded the misleading "Pennsylvania Dutch"; wily, incomprehensibly jabbering Chinamen (aka Celestials). Mostly they were rough caricatures endlessly repeated by writers and performers with no personal knowledge of the people they were lampooning.

Harrigan, on the other hand, knew his characters. He'd grown up with them on the Lower East Side. He was one of them. If his blackface "nagurs" didn't rise much above minstrel show cartoons, songs like "McNally's Row of Flats" are still marvelous and, for the time, unusually humane sketches of Lower East Side slum life in the mid-1800s, with "Bags of rags and papers, / Tramps and other slapers, / Italian lazzaronies, / With lots of other rats, / Laying on the benches, / And dying there by inches / From the open ventilation / In McNally's row of flats."

His "Old Boss Barry" and "Muldoon, the Solid Man" are brilliant portraits of the swaggering Tammany Irishman of the era. Michael Muldoon, introduced in an 1874 sketch at the downtown Theatre Comique, boasted:

I am a man of great influence,
And educated to a high degree,
I came here when small from Donegal,
In the *Daniel Webster*, across the sea;
In the Fourteenth Ward I situated,
In a tenement house with my brother Dan;
By perseverance I elevated,
And went to the front like a solid man.

Go with me and I'll treat you dacent;
I'll set you down and I'll fill the can;
As I walk the street each friend I meet
Says, "There goes Muldoon—he's a solid man."

... I control the Tombs, I control the island,
My constituents they all go there,
To enjoy the Summer's recreation,
And the refreshing East River air;
I'm known in Harlem, I'm known in Jersey,
I'm welcomed hearty on every hand;
Wid my regalia on Patrick's Day,
I march away like a solid man.

Working without Braham on this song, Harrigan set the lyrics to a traditional Irish air. His audiences savored little details, like situating the self-elevating Muldoon in the Fourteenth Ward. Lying between the Bowery and Broadway below Houston Street, it was a rough area but still one rung up the social ladder from the immigrant-stuffed Fourth, Sixth, and Seventh Wards. Not coincidentally, it was also where the Theatre Comique was. They liked that he came over on the *Daniel Webster*, one of the best-known packet ships that made the Liverpool to Boston run in the 1850s—many of them might well have come to America on the same ship. They also enjoyed the political jokes. "Solid Men to the Front" was the title of an 1870 march composed by a Claudio Grafulla and dedicated to Tammany's Boss Tweed, whose corpulently imperial likeness graced the front of the sheet music. (Sousa later copped the title for a different march.) Harrigan premiered "Muldoon, the Solid Man" only a few months after Boss Tweed's downfall, when he was arrested on multiple charges of graft and corruption and sent to the jail on Blackwell's (now Roosevelt) Island "To enjoy the Summer's recreation, / And the refreshing East River air."

A few days before Christmas 1884 Harrigan & Hart's Theatre Comique burned to cinders. Then in May 1885 Hart broke up the duo, to great lamentation among fans and critics. He struggled briefly on his own, but audiences never forgave him. He left the stage and sank into a pitiful physical and mental decline that was written up in all the newspapers as paresis, without mentioning that the cause was tertiary syphilis. He died, prematurely aged at thirty-six, in 1891. Harrigan spoke well of him to reporters but did not attend the funeral.

Harrigan and Braham sailed on, opening the grand new Harrigan's Theatre on Herald Square and touring nationally to great success. But by the late 1890s Harrigan's star was fading too. He had to give up the Herald Square theater, which became Garrick's. Into the early 1900s he toured his greatest hits to dwindling audiences around the country, did some vaudeville, played Uncle Tom in blackface. At his last public appearance in 1910, at a Friends of Ireland dinner, the other diners cheered him with a rendition of the song George M. Cohan had introduced at the Garrick two years earlier, roaring, "H . . . A . . . double R . . . I . . . G-A-N spells HARRIGAN . . ." Born into an Irish stage family in 1878, Cohan had grown up idolizing Harrigan.

Fans and friends formed the Ned Harrigan Club that year. He was too ill to attend their first annual dinner and died, at sixty-six, before their second in 1911. They met for the rest of the decade, wearing green top hats and steak bibs with Dan Mulligan's likeness on them, and singing their way through the Harrigan-Braham songbook. Their membership included a couple of young state assemblymen who'd go on to be two of New York City's most famous politicians: Alfred E. Smith, proud son of the Fourth Ward, later governor and presidential candidate, and Jimmy Walker from the Irish Ninth Ward in Greenwich Village, later mayor. When Smith was introduced at the Democrat's national convention in 1920 he asked the band to play Harrigan and Braham's "Maggie Murphy's Home" as his theme song, but there was a mix-up on the bandstand and they played "The Sidewalks of New York" instead. The substitute became indelibly associated with him.

As the 20th century progressed, Ned Harrigan was largely forgotten. When Jimmy Cagney sang "Harrigan" in the 1942 *Yankee Doodle Dandy*, the movie gave no hint that the song was inspired by an actual hero of Cohan's. A musical called *Harrigan 'n Hart* opened at the Longacre on Broadway in 1985 and closed after only four performances; the cast included *Star Wars'* Mark Hamill as Tony Hart. In 2006, traditional Irish musician and folklorist Mick Moloney, who teaches at NYU, reconstructed some of Harrigan's greatest hits on the album *McNally's Row of Flats*. He cleaned up some of the lyrics and softened the music a bit for sensitive modern ears but preserved the rollicking humor and big heart that wowed listeners a hundred and forty years ago.

5 The Pyramid Club

Clayton

Clayton wrote this for *The Village Sun* in April 2021.

. . .

In April 2021, it was announced that the Pyramid Club on Avenue A was closed due to the pandemic. Gone, finished, shut forever. I was not surprised. What did surprise me is that of all the neighborhood clubs that have disappeared, the ones we heard so much hurt and pain and crying over the loss of—CBGB, Webster Hall, Palladium, the Continental, and on and on—I heard few mentions of the Pyramid Club.

The Pyramid was almost always overlooked, yet it gave birth to so much. The Pyramid opened the door to so many careers and creative opportunities. Certainly for me. For sure. Loved that place.

A little architectural history, from the East Village / Lower East Side Historic District designation report in October 2012: "Peter Doegler briefly operated a brewery at 101 Avenue A from 1859 to 1863 before moving his operations uptown to 55th Street. In 1879–80 he replaced that building with a newer structure designed by another tenement architect, William Jose. For many years the ground floor housed a German bar and meeting hall catering to local residents, and was the site of important meetings of labor groups and a central space for community events. . . . Especially ornate examples of the neo-Grec style can be found at 101 Avenue A."

By the late 1970s, 101 Avenue A was a run-down Polish bar where the local alcoholics came by for their 9 a.m. 50-cent pick-me-up; the brief location of the Nuyorican Poets Café; then a lesbian hangout, with a jukebox, no sound system, under the ownership of Richie Hajguchik. Richie was a mail carrier.

In 1981, Richie was approached by Bobby Bradley, Alan Mace, Victor Sapienza, and John Tucker. They had the brilliant idea of throwing a party in the unused back room, which turned out to be a smashing success.

From that point, the party had started. Brian Butterick came on as the Pyramid's manager.

The low-rent dive bar became a collective of what the Lower East Side represents. The central core was gay, the security was the local skinheads, and the entertainment was a reflection of all the different kinds of explorations that drew creators to the LES.

One art form became a symbol of the club—the Pyramid drag queens. **The drag scene at the Pyramid was typical of the Lower East Side, different from most other underground venues.** Normal drag performers dress up to look like famous movie stars. These performers invented characters, often making use of an art form Kembra Pfahler, of the Voluptuous Horror of Karen Black, called "Availablism." Availablism is making use of anything you have available to make whatever it is you need. Drag was still underground. **RuPaul (who started out at the Pyramid) had not yet dragged drag into the mainstream.**

In 1985, taking photos in front of my front door, I captured Peter Kwaloff, later known as SUNPK. He asked if I would be interested in documenting him getting into character in the Pyramid's dressing room on a Sunday night, preparing for the show "Whispers." Seeing this as a photography adventure, I immediately said yes.

Drag night photos became one of the staples of my photo collection. It was during one of these sessions that I was introduced to Nelson Sullivan. It was a brief introduction that changed my life. Nelson introduced me to the handheld, commercially available video camera. In less than a minute, I understood this tool. A minute, a tool, an idea, a meeting. I got it. Bang. I would go on to use the video camera to document the police riot in Tompkins Square Park in 1988.

A few of the queens I documented: Audrey (Michael London), Mona Lisa (John Kelly), Hapi Phace (Mark Rizzo), Hattie Hathaway (Brian Butterick), Tabboo! (Stephen Tashjian), Picnic Smith (Kwaloff), Lypsinka (John Epperson). I also captured female creators Kathleen and Kennon B Raines.

I met Raybeez, the head of security at the Pyramid. Raybeez was a communicator, a facilitator, a positive voice for the New York hardcore music scene. Ray was the leader, the creator of the band WarZone. Combining what I learned from Nelson with the introductions Ray made, I went on to document many of the period's hardcore bands: Side by Side, Sick of It All, Token Entry, Bad Brains, Murphy's Law, Krack Down, Absolution, Sheer Terror, and more.

I had been curating and doing shows at the Chameleon Club. The Chameleon Club, on East 6th Street between A and B, was the first club to have a large-screen video projection setup. I put together numerous memorial shows, like Steve Bonge and his hot rod, motorcycles, wild lifestyle videos and Charles Gatewood's extreme body modification videos. And I met fascinating bartenders like Edwig.

Ari Roussimoff and I created the Tattoo Society of New York in 1986. We moved the meetings from Uri Kapralov's 6th Sense Gallery to the Chameleon Club, and then, when we needed more space, to the Pyramid Club.

I produced a number of shows at the Pyramid. One memorable show was the "Artists Talk on Art" benefit I did with Bob Wiegand. We presented a large cross section of talents, like Rolando Vega (playing Arleen Schloss), Robert Delford Brown, Taylor Mead, Pamela Stockwell, La Toilette Jackson and Mr. Fashion, Mathew Courtney, Lenny Horowitz, Carolee Schneemann, and others. Another fantastic memory is documenting Wigstock, which grew out of the bowels of the Pyramid.

Later I was blessed to come under the spell of the band DAMEHT, "The Mad" backwards. Rivington Starchild, the band's leader, first came to me to see if I had any photos of his father, a murdered Dominican drug dealer who ran a spot on Rivington Street. Then a number of circumstances brought us back together.

This period with DAMEHT turned out to be a major blessing. In terms of bringing greater attention to my and Elsa's art pieces, Rivington is one of the smartest people I have dealt with. We made a lot happen. I was able to hook them up to play at the Pyramid Club. They put on a number of summer shows. These shows brought back all the thrills and excitement of the old Pyramid Club. It was still the dump it always was, but boy, there was pure magic in those walls.

6 Boris Lurie and NO!art

Clayton and John

In the summer of 1993, Clayton Gallery hosted an art exhibition called "NO!art." It was a small show of maybe a dozen pieces, but there was no missing the tone—ugly and negativist. The painting was intentionally "bad." Messy collages of images ripped from tabloids and old porn were slapped in the viewer's face as angry reminders of everything vulgar and filthy in the world just outside.

When John saw it he told Clayton he thought it was nice of him to give a few punky East Village artists a little space for a show. Clayton explained that yes, the work was East Village all right—but it all dated from 1959 to 1964. As far as he knew, this was the first time any of this work—by Boris Lurie, Isser Aronovici, and Aldo Tambellini—had been shown in the U.S. in almost 30 years.

Clayton had met Boris two years earlier, at a screening of Ari Roussimoff's *Shadows in the City* at Millennium on East 4th Street. He met Harry Smith that night as well. Everybody knew about Harry. But Clayton had never heard of Boris. Few people had at that point.

Clayton introduced John to Boris, and John wrote about him in *NYPress* in February 1994, surely the first press Boris had gotten in America in years. The article began:

> In the bleak winter light filtering through a snow-covered skylight, Boris Lurie's little studio on East 6th Street is almost impassably cluttered with the kind of mess an artist accumulates over 30 years.
> The shadows are dense with rolled canvases, pieces of stretchers, cans of paint, brushes standing in jars, interesting flotsam picked up on the streets, haphazardly stacked drawings, pages torn from magazines, worktables piled with less identifiable junk, a mattress on the floor, a toilet that doesn't look like it works, and over everything that kind of furry, lint-gray dust it takes years of dedicated neglect to build up. All four burners on a little gas stove are lit, but they don't penetrate

either the gloom or the cold. Someone's plumbing upstairs is busted, and there's a steady, desultory drip of brown water through a spot in the ceiling.

Lurie finds a narrow space and a few broken little chairs to settle into. In his late 60s, he has rounded, sad-eyed, Russian-Jewish good looks accentuated by a trim, gray mustache and the soft vestiges of an accent in his speech. He's dressed like a stevedore against the cold, in a wool watch cap and heavy sweater. As we talk we flick our cigarettes into a rusty tin can on the concrete floor between us. It bothers me a little to watch him smoke; he's just been in the hospital for a pacemaker operation...

. . .

NO!art was a moment in art history that art history has chosen to forget. Like the roughly coterminous Pop Art crowd, Lurie and the NO!artists worked with commercial and pop culture imagery. But where Pop Art was essentially the work of ironists exulting in the sleek surfaces of Camelot consumerist culture, the NO!art group burrowed into the dark and cloacal downside of that booster zeitgeist.

NO!artists burned dolls and melted toy soldiers and scrawled NO! like graffiti tag across their canvases. They were pro-Castro and anti-military. They organized group exhibitions with titles like "Doom Show" (protesting JFK's nuclear buildup) and "The American Way of Death," an installation of coffins and mortuary art. They constructed ugly sculptures of smashed televisions and street garbage, desecrated crucifixes and the American flag, and in one infamous show filled an uptown gallery with sculptures that looked like piles of feces—the "Shit Show."

Had it come along later than the '60s, there's little doubt that NO!art would have become some kind of media demon-darling. NO!art did get some press—some of it even mildly supportive—but its ultimate legacy was best summed up by *New York Times* and *Art in America* critic Brian O'Doherty, writing in 1971: *It is extremely difficult to produce a kind of art that histories will pass over in silence, that the art magazines will dismiss, that will embarrass collectors and be offensive to most other artists. [NO!art] succeeded in achieving this large negative.*

Today, the only book devoted to documenting the scene is the one Lurie produced himself with the help of hipster chronicler Seymour Krim. Lurie began it in 1969 and spent two decades failing to find a publisher for it. It finally came out as a fat paperback, simply called *NO!art*, published in Germany in 1988 and never distributed here. The copy loaned to me by Patterson sheds a few more pages every time I open it—more traces vanishing before my eyes.

That Lurie was in New York at all in the 1950s was a bit of a miracle . . .

. . .

Back to the beginning.

Boris Lurie was born into a prosperous Jewish home in Leningrad in 1924. His father, an industrialist, was a businessman who did well even under the Communists. Boris wanted to be an artist from a young age. His father told him he was crazy. "Boris, who's going to buy that shit?"

Papa Lurie moved the family to Riga, Latvia, in 1925. In 1940, Soviet tanks rolled into Riga as the USSR forcibly annexed Latvia. Then, in 1941, Germany invaded and pushed the Soviets out. As the Germans approached, many Jews fled Riga. Apparently Boris's father hesitated, perhaps hedging his bets, maybe thinking that if he could prosper under the Communists he could do the same under the Nazis. He was wrong. The SS rounded up all of Riga's remaining Jews. They kept the males they thought could be put to work, including Boris and his father, and massacred the females, including Boris's mother, grandmother, girlfriend, and one of his two sisters. The other sister escaped to Italy and then the U.S. Boris and his father spent the entire war in various forced labor camps, including Buchenwald-Magdeburg in eastern Germany.

Speaking about it half a century later, Boris was fatalistic. "You are condemned to death, and you know it very well. You try to cheat the fates and play your luck. It's all an accident whether you succeed or not. I guess it helped to have a robust constitution and a certain amount of brains, too, but it was more luck than anything else. It was totally unpredictable."

In 1945, as the Allies penetrated Germany, the camp guards fled. Lurie escaped along with other prisoners, hiding in the woods, pursued by the local police until "finally the Occupation troops arrived." Since he spoke English, he was employed as a translator by U.S. Army counterintelligence. In 1946 he and his father were allowed to come to New York.

"I was very impressed with New York. Especially coming from Germany, which was totally destroyed, the cities completely flattened. The last place we were stationed was near Frankfurt. Frankfurt was nothing, just stones. So to come to New York was a shocking experience."

Still wanting to pursue his art—no doubt to his father's dismay—Boris headed below 14th Street, where artists lived and worked because of the extremely cheap rents. He and an artist friend got a cold water flat on Columbia Street on the Lower East Side.

"We took out the walls and made a studio out of it. It was $15 a month. But no electric at all, no hot water. I was really amazed that in New York they'd have buildings with no electricity. That was the real Lower East Side. I saw the Lower East Side in the very last, short period of its existence. Within a couple of years it was all gone. They all moved to the suburbs or whatever."

Lurie's art, largely self-taught, didn't fit a '50s art scene increasingly dominated by the Abstract Expressionists. His work was figurative as opposed to abstract. His imagery in the early '50s didn't directly address the war and the Holocaust, but it was already showing a grim and abject view of humanity, especially in a series he called "Dismembered Women"—fleshy nudes, somewhere between Rubens and the Venus of Willendorf, with their limbs rearranged. Was he thinking of the women in his family? Boris believed he was making art that socially engaged; the Ab Ex painters wanted to make art that was spiritual, transcendental, and removed.

"Abstract Expressionism became very esoteric and secretive," he remembered. "It was a funny combination of things. On the one hand it was very Existentialist. On the other, they were America Firsters. They wanted to build up an American art, they hated everything European. They talked like longshoremen, a very rough, working-class language. And drinking a lot. And very patriotic Americans at the same time, though most of them had not served in the war. Most of them were 4-Fers. So it was a little contradictory."

The art scene on the Lower East Side was beginning to coalesce around East 10th Street, where cheap storefronts were easily used as galleries, often artist-run co-ops. In one basement on East 10th Street was the March Gallery, "a cooperative gallery that slowly folded, and we took it over. The co-op movement was a terrific thing." Artists showed what they wanted, "and they had their own audience, an audience which wasn't oriented to sales. You'd get the appreciation of your peers based on their own true feelings. It was a great period, but gradually they lost interest.

They wanted to get into the uptown galleries. We took that cooperative idea seriously."

"We" included Sam Goodman, "who originally was an Abstract Expressionist, then he had a conversion and became a sort of social junk sculptor. He went crazy over junk." And Stanley Fisher, "who was originally a poet. He published a book called *Beat Coast East*," which Lurie illustrated. He began to do collages.

It was probably Goodman who pushed Boris to bring his Holocaust experiences to the foreground in his work. Beginning in '59, the three of them organized themed shows and invited other artists to participate. The "Vulgar Show," "Doom Show," the inevitable "NO!Show," and so on. The work was raw, anti-aesthetic and anti-art and anti-pretty-much-everything in ways that were viscerally shocking, sometimes provoking an actual physical response. In one show's introduction, Lurie wrote: *The price for collaboration in art is—as in the concentration camps—excremental suffocation.*

He began doing collages roughly mixing pin-up nudes, porn, and BDSM photos with news photos of piled-up death camp corpses. The porn photos were often ripped and crumpled so that the models look "dismembered" and as brutalized as the camp prisoners. The collages were built up in scabrous layers, the photos slapped down on top of one another as though Lurie had punched them down with his fists. In a horrific one called *Railroad to America*, a buxom cutie pulling down her undies to bare her fleshy buns at the pornographer's camera seems to be rising out of a death camp boxcar overflowing with the gaunt limbs and dull faces of corpses.

The "NO!Show" consisted of that word splashed and stenciled all over paintings, walls, photos of politicians, planks of wood, etc. It prompted a critic to nickname the group's aesthetic NO!art, which stuck. As more artists participated, the shows completely filled up the basement with haphazard environments, a big and spontaneous art mess. Swastikas and hand grenades, torn and defaced posters, newspaper headlines, dead flowers, hundreds of plaster-cast penises, mushroom clouds.

From the article:

For a movement that has vanished from history, it's worth noting that these shows drew healthy crowds. Mostly other artists, but also some pretty high-powered art press—O'Doherty, Dore Ashton, Thomas Hess of *Art News*, Tom Wolfe.

"Everybody came to the March Gallery," Lurie says. "They made the scene. All the Pop artists came." James Rosenquist (*The F-111*) was a friend of some NO!artists; Warhol was there. "They went around looking at what was going on." Some Abstract Expressionists, like de Kooning and Franz Kline, "were very sympathetic personally, but they weren't knocking themselves out to help us." Though Lurie adds that Elaine de Kooning, "in spite of the fact that she was not too sympathetic to what we were doing, conveyed to Hess that this was something important."

How did they all react?

"People were very upset," he replies with a grin. "That went for practically everybody. The Abstract Expressionists didn't like it, and the Pop artists didn't like it. They felt threatened by it on two counts. First, they were all hoping to get into the mainstream, the galleries uptown. They really felt that we were rocking the boat, ruining their chances. And second, they didn't like the social propagandistic aspects of it."

The thing is, had the Lurie crowd aimed more to please than to dismay, the early '60s was a good time for a new, identifiable art movement to make its presence felt in New York.

"The novelty of Abstract Expressionism had given out," Lurie explains. Art investors and promoters "were looking for a new product." Unfortunately for NO!art, "the new product had to be as different as possible, but at the same time not insulting . . . something that is pleasant, that affords good conversation, that's easy to understand."

And that, he says, was Pop.

Like NO!art, Pop was a rejection of Abstract Expressionism's aesthetic purism and otherworldliness; like NO!art, Pop Art imagery came straight out of the real world of fighter jets and sexy advertising and commercial graphics—"but they used it in a contrary sense," Lurie says. "Pop cleaned it up. They made it palatable. Also, Pop had a campy attitude, which we didn't like at all. It was sort of tongue-in-cheek, no politics or social subject matter . . . We always felt that Pop Art was *celebrating* the environment of consumers, not knocking it in any way." In his book he characterizes Pop as *a fitting background for Park Avenue Cocktail parties.*

Agreeing with Wolfe's sarcastic chronicles of that era, Lurie firmly declares that "Pop Art was a 100 percent businesslike promoted project . . . The process of organization I witnessed myself. It was exactly the same as you promote a new stock on the New York Stock

Exchange. The group was assembled, the people who would promote it bought it up at very low prices, and then they promoted it. They were investors."

The main collectors and Medician patrons of Pop—Robert Scull, Leon Kraushaar, Dick Bellamy, names that became legendary in art-money history—were businessmen. They used Leo Castelli's gallery (and Castelli himself came from a business background), but Lurie insists "it wasn't Castelli who started it. People think that's how Pop Art started, because Castelli promoted it. He offered the space, and I guess he liked it, but the real push was by this group of very cold-blooded investors."

And, he says, "They were very smart in promoting it—even as a protest movement. So they had it both ways. They promoted it differently in this country than in Europe. For instance, Andy Warhol had that series of photographs of death chambers. This was not shown here. They showed it in Paris. The people in Paris thought it was social criticism. What was shown here was the cans of soup. They were very careful about how they did that."

On the other hand, he also declares, "After we started NO!art, we really didn't care if we sold anything. And furthermore," he smiles, "we *didn't* sell anything."

. . .

An art collector with the iconic name of Gertrude Stein came to the March Gallery shows and, unlike most other collectors, liked what she saw. But then she was an unusual collector. A New York native, she came from a family tradition of anarcho-syndicalism; the revolutionary Emma Goldman was her godmother.

In 1963 she opened Gallery Gertrude Stein in a basement on 81st near Madison Avenue. She sold things like Kandinsky and Klee out of a back room, but the front space was devoted to bringing NO!art uptown.

Their short reign there culminated in '64 with the "NO!Sculpture Show," aka the "Shit Show." Goodman and Lurie filled the space with what seemed to be piles of excrement—actually, sculptures of plaster extruded from plastic bags and pipes and then realistically painted. All different kinds of shit, from long, firm logs to a mountainous 500 lb. bloody stool to squishy-looking splatters that formed the signature *NO!* logo.

The *New York Times* called it *the ultimate revolution of the subject matter.* People came into the gallery, thought it was real shit, and actually imagined that they could smell the stink.

"Boris, who's going to buy that shit?"

From the article:

When I say to Lurie that the appearance of NO!art must have been something of a bombshell in the uptown gallery environment, he replies, "Yeah, but it was a quiet bombshell. In some instances, when we got reviews it pulled in some people, but otherwise there weren't hordes like we had on 10th Street." And uptown drew a different kind of people, he writes: not artistes, but *a middle-aged crowd of what appeared pleasure-seeking "neurotic" well-off types, a crowd hard to define, amorphous, jelly-like.*

Tom Wolfe noted in his review of the show: *Shocking the bourgeoisie is getting tougher and tougher . . . These people are frustrating. They still won't come right out and be shocked. They, the culturati of the New York art world, look right at the mounds lying there on the floor, and talk about them in terms of the usual, their mass, their tension, their thrust, their plastic ambience and so forth.*

Quite a bombshell.

"The only ones at the time who could help promote our work was that Pop group," Lurie says. "That was Gertrude Stein's home, that they would come in and start to buy something. This was nixed immediately by Scull, who came in and didn't say a word. After he left Gertrude Stein came up to me and said, 'You might as well pack up. Forget about the whole show. Nothing is gonna happen.'"

Then again, when they put on the "Shit Show," Kraushaar "was very interested," Lurie says. "He wanted to buy some pieces." Pop's backers, he claims, wanted to spread out to more galleries "to show that Pop Art is a very wide, popular movement. They were looking for a kind of satellite galleries they could use for second stringers. So Kraushaar had his eye on the Gallery Gertrude Stein. What they would have done, most likely, would be to pick one or two people out of us and help them a little bit, and at the same time squash the whole team."

In his book, he relates that when Kraushaar came up to Goodman and congratulated him personally, Sam Goodman retorted unexpectedly: "I shit on you, too!" A short, self-conscious, aggressive, and defensive man, Kraushaar turned green and walked out.

The "Shit Show" was, perhaps, inevitably, the NO!art group's last excremental fling. *I'd like it understood*, Goodman declared, *this is my final gesture after 30 years in the art world. This is what I think of it.*

"It fell apart," Lurie says. "Gertrude Stein continued on her own with a couple of shows." Lurie became preoccupied by personal and family crises. Goodman died of cancer in '67, his passing unnoted in the press, and "Stanley Fisher went off on a different tack. He got into Zen, organized a commune." He died in 1980. A few NO!art participants found success doing other kinds of art: Dorothy Gillespie, Michelle Stuart, Jerome Rothenberg, Allan Kaprow, the sculptor Kusama.

"I haven't shown in New York ever since then," Lurie says. "In the first place, nobody was chasing after me asking me to show," he laughs. "And I didn't organize anything on my own. I didn't have anybody to work with. I got involved in other areas. And I thought also that it was a totally desperate situation at the time, because the Pop Art had taken over absolutely everything, so there was no hope."

He didn't stop working, and his style is largely unchanged. He has continued to show in Europe, most recently in Cologne in 1988. In Germany, a certain level of interest in and support for NO!art was maintained by the art publishing house Edition Hundertmark, which eventually published Lurie's book *NO!art* and promoted other avant-fringe movements like Fluxus and the controversial Austrian *Aktion* artist Hermann Nitsch. In the U.S., meanwhile, NO!art "was mentioned by certain people, like Lucy Lippard in her book on Pop Art, but basically it totally disappeared."

. . .

Clayton continued to be friends and work with Boris until Boris's death. He adds:

Boris was complex and conflicted. He had secrets, including one bombshell that didn't drop until after he died. He dressed Lower East Side, working class, cheap, like his clothes came from K-Mart, but he carried himself like an aristocrat. There was an elegance to the way he stood, a regal stature, the way he held his cigarette. He'd been born into privilege and wealth, after all, and it showed. You pictured him in a tux looking around the ballroom. Dash Snow had a similar affect. He could walk into the Whitney wearing torn jeans and a ripped-up jacket, but his body language said he deserved to be there, and he always got in. Boris had that. Not arrogance, but a self-assured presence.

When Boris and his father arrived in New York, his father invested in real estate. Boris was handsome, young, the rich man's son. They called him Boris the Lion. He had a German shepherd, drove a sports car, went around with an aristocratic French woman, very elegant, who was in the upper echelons in fashion or advertising.

When Boris's father died in 1964 he left Boris a building on East 77th Street on the Upper East Side. That's something Boris did not reveal to John as they huddled in his East 6th Street studio. He also didn't tell him that he actually lived in an apartment on East 66th Street just off Madison Avenue. It was the Upper East Side, the wealthiest neighborhood in Manhattan, about as far from the Lower East Side as you could get. But his apartment was as cluttered and unkempt as the studio. All kinds of paperwork plastered on the wall and stacked up around an old typewriter. More tin cans for ashtrays. Stove blackened from years of use without ever being cleaned. Rust stain in the porcelain sink from a drip that had dripped for years. Mice running in and out from under the bed, which was hardly ever changed. An old couch and a little tv in the living room. Everything impoverished and degraded. It was like he was re-creating a barracks in a forced labor camp.

I don't think he was playing the starving artist, but he did feign being poor. He pinched pennies until they hollered. He lived like a man of no means. Dinner for him was a can of sardines. He permitted no luxury in his life. I think he was living in the forced labor camp in his head. It was a prison survival lifestyle.

But he really was conflicted. As much as he acted like he rejected the mainstream art world, he got very excited in 1993 when a curator of the Whitney Museum's upcoming "Abject Art" group show contacted him about including a few of his pieces. Boris got the pieces organized, and then somehow, the way I understood it, the Whitney never came to collect them. I put together a NO!art show in my gallery. It ran at the same time as the Whitney one.

And there's this: You know who else lived on East 66th Street? Andy Warhol. He lived a few doors down from Boris. To me that suggests that as much as Boris railed against Pop Art, at least a part of him wanted that success, wanted to be in that crowd. I think he was always hedging his bets, the way his father had.

He didn't preserve his own art. When the curator Estera Milman was planning the Boris exhibition that would be mounted in Iowa in 1999, they found his artwork crammed into the basement of the 66th Street building. A lot of it was stuck together because water had been dripping on it, because Boris rarely fixed the pipes or anything else. His friend Dietmar Kirves came over with his son. Dietmar is an artist who'd worked with Joseph Beuys before meeting Boris in 1978. Boris and Dietmar were very deeply kindred spirits. Dietmar is a very German, very hard-edged anarchist of the old school, no compromise. He hooked Boris up with Edition Hundertmark and designed his book, then got into an argument with the publisher and cut his name out of the acknowledgments, leaving a blank space. That's Dietmar. Dietmar understands the NO!art philosophy implicitly and was instrumental in inspiring Boris to continue it. He and his son spent a lot of time separating the works and repairing them. In 1999 Dietmar started the NO!art website, an extraordinarily deep and meticulous archive of everything and everyone associated with the movement (https://no-art.info/index.html). Boris declared Dietmar the director of NO!art's eastern headquarters, me its western HQ.

In the mid-1990s, when I was traveling in Germany and Austria with the Wildstyle & Tattoo festival I helped organize, I went to Stuttgart to buy a stack of NO!art books from Edition Hundertmark. Boris asked me to take a copy to the director of the Pompidou Center. I took a night train from Berlin to Paris, met this gentleman, handed him the book, explained briefly about Boris and NO!art. He was very gracious, considering that he must have been thinking what the hell. I took a train straight back to Berlin.

I also went to Buchenwald for Boris, to reconnoiter it for an exhibition of Boris's art. The director of Buchenwald Memorial, Dr. Volkhard Knigge, walked me around the camp and I sized up the exhibition space.

I should point out that I did all this on my own dime. Boris never offered to reimburse me for any of it.

In late 1998 I flew with Boris to Germany for the opening of his show at the Buchenwald Memorial, "Boris Lurie: Works 1946–1998." The Memorial must have paid for our airfare. I know Boris didn't. We stayed in the captain's quarters. Buchenwald was cleaned up but it wasn't dressed up yet. East Germany was still deep in debt and going through lots of other problems. If you visit the concentration camp memorials now, I'm not saying it's like going to Macy's, but they're much more fixed up than they were then.

Boris strutted around Buchenwald like the returning victor. He was in high spirits, swaggering, Boris the strongman, Boris the invincible. "I'm back, you fuckers!" He was delighted to see they had his old prisoner serial number, 95966, on the wall. "Look, Clayton, that's me!" The show was his triumphant return, his triumph over the Nazis, over death, and he made them pay and pay. It was the most difficult and expensive show they'd ever mounted there.

Then came the day, one of the most unforgettable of my life, when I watched all that swagger, all that bravado get crushed out of him. It wasn't at Buchenwald, but at Dora, a camp nearby, where prisoners were used as slave labor to build Wernher von Braun's V-2 rockets in the mine shafts. It was a cold, damp, morbid day, fog shrouding the trees, a single railroad car like the ones they used to transport prisoners. We were met by a young former East German guy, a cliched intellectual, skinny, long white fingers, in a trenchcoat. He led us around, describing the inhuman things that went on there in heavy, depressing, Edgar Allan Poe detail. He took us into the mountain. It was even damper and colder in there, oppressively gloomy, with incandescent lights strung up overhead on their wires, like a construction site.

The young man went on about how many thousands of prisoners died inside this mountain working on the rockets. And as he talked, I watched the weight of it all crush Boris. It penetrated his psyche. He'd always had this steely discipline, this defense in his mind that let him talk about the Holocaust and make his ugly art without betraying emotion, much less weakness. I watched it crumble that day in the mine, and he was never the same after that. It was like he was shell-shocked. After this he started breaking down physically—his legs started to go; he had his first stroke. Something had fractured in his head and broken his spirit. He had lost his imperviousness. We've all known older people who were powering along, doing fine, and then something happens—a trip on the stairs, say. It shakes their confidence, and suddenly they're an old person. They lose their spirit, their drive. I think that's what happened to Boris. Everything about the inside of that mountain was the perfect environment to make that happen.

His health deteriorated a lot in his last few years. He died in 2008. That's when his biggest secret of all came to light. When he died, Boris the cheap, penniless artist left an estate worth $80 million! He'd made it playing penny stocks on Wall Street. Eighty million dollars! Eating sardines out of the can. Living in squalor.

Maybe he never escaped the forced labor camp after all.

Dietmar and I continue to keep the spirit of NO!art alive as an international movement, as you can see from Dietmar's website. Gertrude Stein runs the Boris Lurie Art Foundation to promote his work and legacy.

7 Linda Twigg

Clayton

Linda Twigg was a downtown legend, another complex character with many sides. She was pretty and petite, a blue-eyed blonde, a devout Catholic of the old school, a benefactor and friend to the creative community, a host of great parties where interesting people met. But she was also, as the photographer Louis Cartwright put it, a "gangsterette." She was a major player in the downtown pot world, got into much harder drugs herself, was involved in gambling, carried a gun, and if she thought you crossed her she'd make you very sorry. It all turned out to be a tragic combination.

Linda worked for a big-name pot dealer named Bruno. Being small, she had a bodyguard, Anne Ardolino, aka Anntelope. Anne was a poet with a ton of street knowledge, who got by for a long time as a bottom-end streetwalker, a five-dollar-blowjob hooker. She had an unusual attitude about it. She looked at it as a humanitarian thing, healing and bringing comfort to men.

Linda was also in the gambling business. She sold clay chips to the casinos. She had a machine that embossed the value and the casino's logo onto them. You had to have a license to do that. I once saw pink chips worth $1,000 each. She also made some for Mickey the Pope that had his sickle-and-pot insignia stamped on them. You'd buy a $100 chip from Mickey and use it later to buy pot from him. She once got an order for some from the Bush family, to be sent to their summer retreat at Kennebunkport, Maine.

Linda rented a room in the Chelsea that she used as a game room. Her main game was poker. This was a quiet, small, private, invitation-only game. It was there that you really saw the way she supported creative people. There were portraits on the walls of Ginsberg, Burroughs, Candy Darling. She had a large collection of books of downtown and Beat literature. Since she lived on the Lower East Side, not in the hotel, she let Herbert Huncke stay there. His job was to keep the place clean, oversee the games, handle orders, and sometimes follow up on one of Linda's unusual demands. Herbert, one the original Beats, was credited with coining the name Beat. He was the guide who opened the door to much of the illicit world the naive Beat writers (Kerouac, Ginsberg et al.) so desperately sought to enter. Huncke also has the undistinguished reputation of being the one who turned William Burroughs on to junk.

When Huncke's autobiography *Guilty of Everything* was published in 1990, Linda honored his moment with a book-signing party in her Chelsea room. The place was filled with many underground creative-world luminaries: Bob Fass of WBAI's Radio Unnamable, Roger Richards of Greenwich Village's Rare Book Room, Huncke's friend Louis Cartwright, the opium poet Marty Matz, poet and shaman Ira Cohen, filmmaker Jamie Rasin, writer Jeremiah Newton, and others. At other parties there you'd see Mickey the Pope, Robert Frank, Harry Smith. She was a real facilitator that way.

Then there was the side of Linda that was hard as a brick wall. Her reputation was that if she thought you cheated her or ripped her off she'd make you pay. Maybe it was because she was so small, she wanted everyone to know not to mess with her. This side of her turned disastrous and deadly.

Around 1993 she took on a boyfriend, David Degondea. He was around 21, ten years or so younger than her. He was a funny sort of character to be on that scene. He was from New Jersey, a clean-cut frat boy type. Linda decided to groom him to be more of a gangster. They'd be walking down the street and a panhandler would hit her up for spare change. She'd rag on David, "How could you let that guy hit on me like that? Why didn't you shoot him?" Apparently it worked. Once, when Linda told David that a guy who worked for her was stealing from her, he stormed over to the guy's place and gave him a savage beating.

I think she regretted that. She was a very old-school Catholic, very into the saints, like Saint Dismas, the "good thief" crucified along with Jesus. When she did something wrong she repented, confessed, lit candles, said novenas, all that. I think being responsible for that beating really weighed on her soul.

At that point they were living on East 1st Street between First and Second Avenues. She started using her own homemade formula of GHB, the club drug, and it was really screwing with her mind. Homemade GHB! Toxic, toxic stuff. She started quarreling with the heroin dealers upstairs, which had David tweaked to a very high level of anxiety. He came to me and said, "Clayton you have to talk to Linda. We have to calm down this fight with the heroin dealers."

I went to Eddie Arce, a Puerto Rican guy born in the neighborhood, who had a small storefront on 1st Street where he silkscreened sports logos on t-shirts and other merchandise. I figured he'd know the heroin dealers and might be able to help. Instead, it turned out Eddie and Dave had set up a big deal where they were going to meet a couple of buyers at the shop and sell them a few pounds of pot and some guns for something like $50,000.

The two buyers come in, check the merchandise, go back out to the car to get the money—then burst back in, guns drawn. Dave and Eddie think they're being robbed. Dave shoots and kills one of the guys, Luis Lopez.

They were undercover cops. The deal had been a setup. The cops who arrested Dave and Eddie beat the hell out of both of them. In 1995, Dave was sentenced to 25 years to life for killing Lopez, 25 years to life for the attempted murder of his partner, and 5 to 15 years each for criminal possession of a gun and marijuana. He's not eligible for parole until 2047. Eddie got 2 to 6 years for selling pot and a firearm. Even the guy who worked in the back, who had nothing to do with any of this, was arrested.

But not Linda. The cops had to know who she was and that she was right down the street, but curiously they never got a warrant and busted in on her. I've always wondered about that.

Linda's mental and physical state deteriorated after that. She lived in a few of the Lower East Side's squats. One of them was Glass House, an abandoned glass factory on East 10th Street and Avenue D. Margaret Morton, the photographer and Cooper Union professor, did a book about it. Linda was carrying a gun at that stage, a big, old-fashioned silver pistol, and the rest of the squatters were very scared of her.

The drug use really messed with her. It was tragic. Along with the home-brewed GHB, she started shooting heroin. She'd lose consciousness, fall and hit her head on the edge of a table. Her face would be swollen and black and blue, her nose smashed. She'd wind up in the hospital sometimes, where she did not want to be because she'd be jonesing soon. So she'd tell them, "I'm going to call my lawyer Ron Kuby, because you do not have the right to keep me here." They'd send her home. She used to call me and Elsa when she was freaking out and we'd go over to her place. Once I managed to get her to the Bellevue emergency ward. That wasn't easy, because she'd threaten to shoot me, and knowing her, I believed she would. I told the doctor he had to commit her to the psych ward, because otherwise she'd walk. He said to me, "Well, why did you beat her up?" I explained that I was just a friend, that she looked so beat-up because of the drugs and falling down. He didn't buy it and she got out again.

One day when I was out of town she was really doing poorly, maybe from an OD, and called Elsa. Elsa went over there and called an ambulance. It was too late. Linda died that day.

8 The Cradle of Hollywood

John

John wrote a version of this for *The Chiseler*.

. . .

In the second half of the 20th century, the Lower East Side was a bubbling cauldron of film and video creativity that changed the world of cinema. The book *Captured*, edited by Clayton, documents the rich variety of scenes and players associated with the neighborhood in those decades. To name a few: Jack Smith, Harry Smith, Taylor Mead, Beth B, Jim Jarmusch, Ira Cohen, Steve Buscemi, Rosario Dawson, Nick Zedd, Jonas Mekas, Emile de Antonio, Eric Bogosian, Luis Guzman, Larry Fessenden, Ann Magnuson, Amos Poe, Richard Kern. It's absolutely no coincidence that Jonas's Anthology Film Archives, the national storehouse for avant-garde and experimental film, is in the neighborhood.

But the neighborhood has a longer history in film, back to the very birth of the movies. It's no exaggeration to say that without the Lower East Side there would not have been a Hollywood.

By the 1920s Hollywood was well established as the capital of the American film industry, but many of the talents who made that happen—in front of the camera, behind it, and in the business offices—were transplanted New Yorkers. For the quarter of a century or so that the movie business was in its infancy, the New York metro area was its cradle. And no part of New York played a larger role in nurturing the infant than the Lower East Side.

. . .

The movie industry evolved in stages. For all their immense impact on popular culture later, movies started out humbly, and for a while it looked like they might never be more than a minor amusement. The first movies shown to the American public, Edison's Kinetographs, were unveiled in New

York City in 1894. Because no one had yet invented a viable movie projector, the first short Kinetograph film loops—twenty to sixty seconds—weren't shown on screens. One viewer at a time dropped a penny in a peep show machine, which Edison called a Kinetoscope, and watched the loop through an eyepiece. The peep—aka "penny vaudeville"—spread mostly in amusement arcades like the ones around Union Square, where it shared floor space with slot machines, test-your-strength machines, and other time-frittering novelties aimed at a clientele that was almost exclusive men and boys. Given this setting, it's no surprise that many of the reels were risqué, with titles like *A Busy Day at the Corset Models'* and *The Boarding House Bathroom*.

Peeps never caught on in a big way, but luckily the first working film projectors came along in 1896. New Yorkers were the first Americans to see films projected on screens: at the Keith-Albee Union Square Theatre; at Koster and Bial's Music Hall on 34th Street, where Macy's is now; and at Oscar Hammerstein's opulent new Olympia Theater complex in Longacre (later Times) Square. For almost a decade Americans would mostly see films screened as part of a bill in vaudeville theaters, known in the business as a "pick-vaud" combo.

Those first short silents were an immediate hit, and Edison and others rushed to supply the burgeoning new market. Although Edison, as was his wont, sought monopolistic dominance, he had stiff competition at first from the French Lumiere brothers and from one of his own former employees—W. K. L. Dickson, who'd done the bulk of the work developing the Kinetograph. Dickson abandoned Edison in 1895 and helped start American Mutoscope & Biograph, the first moving picture studio in Manhattan. It was located in the Roosevelt Building, built by Teddy's family, which still stands at Broadway and East 13th Street, just a block south of Union Square (and today, fittingly, across the street from a multiplex). Biograph shot its films up on the roof to take advantage of natural sunlight. Actors played in front of a one-wall backdrop, everything else open to the sky, and the set could be turned to follow the sun. Biograph used performers from nearby vaudeville theaters, so the subject matter was largely the same: pretty girls in tights, slapstick, ethnic jokes. Later Biograph moved to a converted brownstone on 14th Street, and later still to a studio in the Bronx, with D. W. Griffith as its star director.

The next evolutionary step came in 1903, when Edwin S. Porter shot *The Great Train Robbery* for Edison in New Jersey. It had its world premiere, so to speak, on the Lower East Side, at Hubert's Dime Museum on East 14th Street. By the following week it was showing in a dozen venues in the city, and from there spread around the country, American moviemaking's first bona fide box office smash.

By the appearance two years later of the first makeshift movie houses, called nickelodeons (for the usual 5-cent admission), the New York market was well primed. "Nickel madness" spread with amazing speed. The first nickelodeon opened in Pittsburgh in 1905, showing *The Great Train Robbery*. By 1910 there were about 200 nickelodeons in Manhattan, attracting 1.5 million New Yorkers a week, a quarter of the city's entire population. A third of them were on or around the Lower East Side, which took to this new amusement like no other neighborhood in the city—in fact, it had the highest concentration of nickelodeons in the U.S. They were not yet full-fledged cinemas. Most were bare-bones conversions of rented storefronts and music halls strung along the Bowery and other avenues from Union Square down. They offered wooden benches or chairs and few amenities, and they represented the cheapest entertainment in the neighborhood—cheaper than vaudeville, burlesque, a night out dancing or drinking, or a day at Coney Island. Like vaudeville, they ran continuous shows from morning till late at night, and for a nickel or dime you could "stay as long as you like."

Critically for the Lower East Side audience, the silent films presented no language barriers. A 1908 report on nickelodeon audiences in the city noted, "On the Bowery we have seen Chinamen, Italians and Yiddish people, the young and old, often entire families, crowded side by side." The Golden Rule Theater, a nickelodeon on Rivington Street, was said to be drawing 14,000 customers a week in 1907. Amenable to both families and the single working girl, nickelodeons became ad hoc community centers where neighbors met up and socialized. Mothers used them like daycare centers, dropping their kids off while they went about their chores. The abundance of unsupervised youth in working-class nickelodeons scandalized the city's social reformers and moral watchdogs, who railed against the establishments for promoting truancy, delinquency, and loose sexual activity.

By 1915 the nickelodeon had faded away as quickly as it had bloomed. It had done its job of getting Americans to adopt movie going as a favorite pastime, and now it was replaced by actual movie theaters showing feature films.

. . .

Three men from the Lower East Side who started out operating nickelodeons and arcades went on to be pioneering moguls of Hollywood: Adolph Zukor (Paramount), Marcus Loew (Loew's Inc./MGM), and William Fox (Fox Film Corporation, later Twentieth Century Fox). They all started with nearly nothing, had only a modicum of formal education and, many would say, not much taste. What they saw in film early on was its money making potential, and they played central roles in making movies mass entertainment.

Zukor was a Hungarian Jew who came to the Lower East Side at the age of 16 in 1889. He labored in the upholstery and fur trades for a few years, then moved to Chicago, where he started his own fur business. He came back to New York in 1903 and opened an arcade, Automatic Vaudeville, on 14th Street near Union Square. The writer Upton Sinclair would remember it as "one of the sights of the town" with its 5-cent "phonographs, punching bags, weighing machines, chewing-gum machines," and Kinetoscope peep shows. It made a big impression on both Loew and Fox.

Marcus Loew was born in 1870 at Avenue B and East 5th Street, in what was then known as Kleindeutschland, Little Germany, or Dutchtown. His father, recently emigrated from Vienna, worked as a waiter. Marcus began hawking newspapers on the street at age 6 to help the family make ends meet; by 9 he'd quit school to work 6 days a week at a printing plant. He earned 35 cents a 10-hour day. Soon he and a young partner were running their own small printing business and putting out a weekly shopper, the *East Side Advertiser*. By the mid-1890s he was a partner in a fur company, Baer & Loew, operating from a loft on Union Square.

When Zukor opened Automatic Vaudeville, it was right around the corner from Baer & Loew. Loew decided to get into the business himself. He briefly partnered with Zukor, they fell out, and he went off on his own. He opened his first arcade, called People's Vaudeville, in a storefront on East 23rd Street in 1905. He was on his way to building a chain of arcades in New York and other cities when he visited a nickelodeon in the Midwest and saw the future. Returning to New York, he converted People's Vaudeville to a nickelodeon. He also experimented with another type of amusement using film, called the scenic tour. A storefront was made up to look like the inside of a rail car. Films of passing scenery—the Grand Canyon, the Rhine valley—played outside the windows, "while some trick machinery beneath the car was joggling and swaying the whole shebang to give a pretty fair illusion of being on a real railway journey," a contemporary wrote. The idea spread to amusement parks, which have rides today that are not significantly different in concept, just higher-tech. Pretty soon

Loew was building a chain of combination film-and-vaudeville houses, mostly on the East Coast at first. On the Lower East Side, his giant Loew's Delancey Street would screen films continuously from 1912 into the late 1970s. Loew's Canal Street Theatre, opened at 31 Canal Street in 1927, was one of the largest in the city, with a boisterously ornate terra-cotta facade. It showed movies into the 1950s, and the city designated the facade a landmark in 2010. Loew's State Theatre in Times Square, opened in 1921, was one of the most popular movie-and-vaudeville palaces in the city. New Yorkers decided that Loew's should be pronounced *low-eez*, and you still meet some older ones who do. Loew ran his growing empire from nondescript offices above the State that *Fortune* would describe in 1938 as "modest to the point of dinginess." They reflected his careful, relatively conservative business style. Zukor's Paramount theater-and-office building nearby, completed in 1927, was twice as tall and ten times as flashy. Loew would go on to build a chain of some 120 movie palaces around the country, displaying an excellent eye for both choice real estate and prime entertainment markets—such that while Loew's was far from the biggest theater chain around, it was one of the most profitable and stable.

Of all the self-made moguls, no one started lower or faced a steeper climb than William Fox. Born Wilhelm Fried to German Jewish parents in Hungary in 1879, Fox was brought to the Lower East Side when he was 9 months old. The family was very poor and started out in a backhouse behind a tenement on Stanton Street. All the tenants used the outhouse in the cramped courtyard, and Wilhelm grew up with the stink in his nostrils. Like most kids in the neighborhood, his childhood was short. Before he was 10 he was contributing to the family's income by going door to door through the tenements selling 5-cent cans of stove blacking. "To have the stove well blacked was important to the family dignity," his biographer Upton Sinclair explains, "because the kitchen served as the dining room, and also as a reception room for guests."

Will also sold penny packages of lozenges on the streets and in the parks. By the age of 10 he had organized other boys into his own lozenge-peddling empire. He'd buy the lozenges wholesale and pass them out to the kids in his employ. He earned as much as $12 on a good week. It was more than his father made. He quit day school when he was 11 to take a job in the garment industry but went to night school classes for a few years. By 13 he was a foreman at a clothing firm, running a crew of a dozen men and boys who cut linings. With Will earning, the family could move up to a 6-room cold water flat on Rivington Street.

He was 20 when Admiral Dewey, the hero of the Spanish–American War, sailed into New York harbor in September 1899. The city threw a gigantic victory celebration, including a parade all the way from Grant's Tomb to Washington Square. The Library of Congress has Edison footage of Dewey in full regalia leading the march of sailors, soldiers, and marines. Will withdrew all the money he'd been saving up since he was 10 years old, about $500, and invested it in items to peddle to the crowd of onlookers—pretzels, sandwiches, soda pop, and soapboxes they could stand on. The morning of the parade he marshaled his troops and went uptown. But the weather was chill, so no one wanted soda pop, and windy, so they didn't want to be blown off the soapboxes. The dust and grime the wind kicked up ruined the unwrapped sandwiches. All that was left to sell was the pretzels (which, he told Sinclair, Lower East Side kids pronounced *bretzels*). Facing financial ruin and stiff competition from all the other pretzel crews, Will told people that an Admiral Dewey souvenir was baked into every one of his. By the time the customer discovered it was a lie, Fox and his crew had moved on. He sold out his stock and made a small profit. He would resort to that sort of mildly unscrupulous humbug again in his career.

Inspired by Automatic Vaudeville, Fox soon opened his own coin-op arcade in a storefront near Flushing Avenue in Brooklyn. Then, when nickelodeons began sprouting up everywhere, he installed a 150-seat one on the floor above. Brooklynites didn't know from motion pictures yet, so he hired a sidewalk barker to entice them in and up the stairs. He got partners to go in with him on opening more than a dozen other nickelodeons in Brooklyn and Manhattan. Then he began buying actual theaters to present a pick-vaud program. His first was a space in Brooklyn so dilapidated locals called it Bum Theatre; he fixed it up and called it the Comedy.

In 1908 he rented the Dewey Theater on 14th Street, installed a two-hour program combining short films and vaudeville acts, and charged a 10-cent admission. The Dewey was an early avatar of the plush movie palaces to come, with nice seats and uniformed ushers, and it was a huge success. Fox was making movie going safe and attractive for the middle class who had stayed away from the rowdy, smelly nickelodeons. He also rented the Academy of Music across the street to show movies. In 1921 the Prince of Wales, later King Edward VIII, would come to the Academy, meet Fox, and enjoy a program of comic short films that included one with an all-canine cast.

. . .

As movie screens popped up everywhere, sometimes more than one to a city block, a serious shortage in product developed. Theater managers often found that they and their nearby competitors were all screening the same films. So Zukor, Fox, and Loew all turned to producing and distributing their own films. Zukor started the Famous Players Film Company in 1912. Within a few years he merged Famous Players with a few other companies to create what became Paramount Pictures. In the early 1920s Loew acquired the film production houses Metro Pictures, Goldwyn Pictures, and Mayer Pictures to create MGM. One of his financial backers was the gangster Arnold Rothstein.

By 1913 Fox had built an empire of more than 100 theaters and began making his own pictures to put into them. He discovered one of the first movie starlets, Theda Bara, a tailor's daughter from Cincinnati whose real name was Theodosia Goodman. His publicity man invented the backstory that she was Arabic and came up with her stage name, Arab spelled backwards. He arranged her first press conference, at which she dressed like a harem girl and didn't say a word because she wasn't supposed to know English. The ruse worked just as well as Fox's souvenir pretzels once had. The first Fox pictures were shot in a rented studio in Fort Lee, New Jersey. He also shot on Staten Island and in Manhattan.

Edison sought to exert some kind of dominance over what had become an exploding and chaotic movie industry. He launched thousands of patent-infringement lawsuits in all directions. But the exponentially expanding film industry just grew too big too fast for him to control it all.

By 1915 Fox and the others were beginning to build studios in Hollywood, drawn by the year-round sunshine, the variety of outdoor locations, and the cheap real estate. The advent of talking pictures in the later 1920s would cap Hollywood's rise and noisy New York's decline as a film production center. The moguls organized Hollywood along a basic industrial model, vertically integrated, with production, distribution, and exhibition all working together in well-oiled corporate machines. The studios mass-produced the product; the theater chains acted like any other chain stores; and the distribution units kept them efficiently stocked.

By the end of the 1920s, five major companies dominated the American film industry. Three of them were products of the Lower East Side: Paramount, Loew's Inc./MGM, and Fox. Warner Bros. and RKO were the other two.

9 Father Pat

John

John wrote this for *NYPress* in July 1994.

. . .

On the front door of Bonitas House, a brownstone just east of Tompkins Square Park at 606 East 9th Street, is one of those bless-all-those-who-enter-this-house placards. Across the street a wall is tagged with graffiti: *Free Fr. Pat*. A latino teen, tattooed and polite, lets me into the dim foyer. A few other adolescent boys, latino and white, hang around among the secondhand furnishings in the darkened, book-lined parlor. A white-haired grandmother who looks like an ad for the Old Country—anybody's Old Country—sits at a dining table, a teacup near her hand, and silently watches me.

Father Patrick Maloney's small office is in the back, next to the monkish, closet-sized cell where he sleeps. Gray-bearded and pinkish, 62 years old, Fr. Pat—like the graffiti artist, everyone seems to call him that—looks small and childlike in the tall chair behind the used wooden desk. On the wall behind him there's a clock shaped like Ireland, some reproduction Greek Orthodox icons of Jesus and Mary, and a string-art Celtic cross. More teacups on the desk. And more bookshelves, where editions of the Bible, the Koran, the Torah lean with vaguely disturbing chumminess against militant-looking books and tracts about the IRA and the Troubles in Northern Ireland.

Hung from one bookshelf, looking oddly out of place, is some electronic apparatus, hi-tech black, that I take at first for some kind of FM or CB antenna. It's hooked to what looks like a cable tv box.

What it is is Fr. Pat's electronic guard, keyed to a transmitter he wears on his ankle. With a bemused, slightly martyred smile he hikes up his priestly black pants leg to show this to me. Guardian Technologies, it says. It looks like a transistor radio strapped to the white skin above his thin black sock.

If Fr. Pat and his Guardian stray out of range of the equipment hanging from his bookshelves, alarms go off somewhere and his bail bondsman breaks out in a sweat. Because Fr. Pat is under house arrest at 606 East 9th Street, facing federal criminal charges in connection with one of the biggest and oddest Brinks robberies in history.

. . .

In January '93, $7.4 million in cash was stolen from a Brinks facility in Rochester, NY. Among the men arrested and charged in the case almost a year later, one was an Irish-American ex-cop and Brinks watchman. One was an Irishman who was in this country as an undocumented alien. And one was Fr. Pat. (A fourth man, also Irish, was charged later.)

Given these guys' backgrounds, it was no great leap for the FBI and the press to assume that the Brink's job had been an attempt to do a bit of quick and dirty fundraising for the Provisional Irish Republican Army back home. Thomas O'Connor, the inside man, had been active in NORAID, doing more traditional fundraising for the Cause. The FBI didn't buy his story of how armed, ski-masked robbers had pulled the heist. Their investigations led last November to a raid of two Jackson Heights apartments connected to a man named Samuel Ignatius Millar.

In the early '80s, Millar had done prison time in Northern Ireland for explosives and firearms violations. He had in fact been one of "the Blanket Men," the prisoners who went on literal sit-down strikes and fasts in refusal to cooperate with their British jailers, a series of protests that culminated in Bobby Sands's much publicized fasting to death. Millar had allegedly sneaked into the U.S. in '84 with O'Connor's help.

According to the feds, Millar spent the months between the January heist and his November arrest opening a $25,000 bank account with cash, buying money orders, and paying for a trip to Hawaii with stacks of $20 bills. He'd also been observed, they say, going in and out of an apartment in Manhattan, on 1st Avenue, carrying duffel bags literally bulging with cash.

Fr. Pat was allegedly observed going in and out with him. And Fr. Pat has a history of his own. In 1982 he and his brother John, who had an Irish-American import-export business, had been arrested in Ireland on charges of trying to smuggle weapons from the United States.

The November raids in Queens and on 1st Avenue yielded so much cash the feds couldn't count it at first; they simply announced that "hundreds of pounds" of bills had been recovered. They later said it amounted to about half of the $7.4 million. At the 1st Avenue apartment they reported also finding a money counting machine and a tally sheet listing about $1.5 million broken down by denomination. They also raided Bonitas House and the next-door apartment where Fr. Pat's brother lives with his family.

O'Connor, Millar, and Fr. Pat were arrested and indicted on charges of knowingly receiving, possessing, and concealing stolen federally insured funds. Charles McCormack, whose name was on the 1st Avenue lease, was arrested January of 1993. The trial, originally slated to begin in a Rochester federal court that month, was postponed until mid-September.

After a long weekend in Manhattan Correctional Center last November, Fr. Pat was released on $1 million bail, wearing his Guardian. At first he was under strict house arrest, not allowed to leave the building. After a few months, that was loosened so that he's free to move around within the confines of Manhattan, 6 a.m.–9 p.m., and with prior permission can go elsewhere to pursue his priestly duties—trips to a nursing home in Yonkers, to a funeral in Florida, and so on.

"I'm not only not guilty, I'm innocent," Fr. Pat tells me. "There's a difference, you know."

The distinction he's drawing, between mere legality and a higher morality, goes some way to explain the complexity of the man—and, maybe, how he's ended up in his current predicament. When speaking about doing "the Lord's work," he can be almost inaudibly soft-spoken, his words dropping gently as dove's eggs onto the mossy green carpet of his Irish accent. But when he gets to topics of passionate concern for him—things like oppression, racism, and the British "occupation" of Northern Ireland—an angry, defiant Fr. Pat emerges with startling ease.

In the neighborhood around East 9th Street, where he's been doing good works for almost 40 years, he's regarded as something of a saint. Without question, Fr. Pat is dedicated to the people he serves—*fiercely* dedicated, not just to the people, you sense, but to his ideas about them and what they represent. A fierce dedication to your ideas about people is called politics. And even when doing good works, there's been a marked streak of independence and even rebelliousness in Fr. Pat's methods.

Bonitas (Latin for "good") Youth Services was begun in 1957 by some students at St. John's University. They included Pat Moloney, a young seminarian. "I'd just come from Ireland the year before, and I felt that I didn't have much grounding in cultural aspects of American life." The group—which would eventually call itself the Lazarus Community after the man Jesus raised from the dead—set up a storefront operation at 713 East 9th Street between Avenues. C and D, working with the "ragamuffin" kids and their families in the neighborhood.

"They were migrants from Puerto Rico or the Deep South, and I was an immigrant, so we had something in common," Fr. Pat recalls. "And there's nobody better to show you around than the unbiased minds of children."

Fr. Pat would complete his seminary studies in the early '60s, but for years "put on the back burner, much to the distress of my parents, my goal of ordination into the priesthood. I felt that what needed to be done was not the clergy, not the rabbis, not the priests, not the ministers out there doing the work of the Lord. You have to have your ordinary, common people." So "just plain Pat Moloney . . . and a bunch of other lads, we all got together and said, 'We *are* the Church. We can do this work.'"

He calls himself "a democratic Christian communist who believes in the commonality of Man in the best sense of the word." Early on, that spirit attracted the support of Dorothy Day, founder of the Catholic Worker. In 1960, another supporter lent them the use of a Civil War–era house on 14 acres in rural New Jersey. Using surplus and donated materials, the kids and volunteers fixed up the house, filled it with books and educational aids, cleared the property, set up pup tents, and had themselves a summer camp.

"These were tough, New York City street ghetto kids," Fr. Pat recalls. "Some of them budding gang members, Irish, Italian, German, Jews, Hispanic, black . . . When I'd get them out there they were literally transformed." Some are "now grandfathers in this neighborhood."

The winter of '61, the house mysteriously burned down, with everything they'd brought to it. There were rumors that it might have been torched by locals who hadn't liked having the city kids around.

The story made local and then national tv news, attracting donations and swelling the group's volunteer base from "10 or 20 to a couple hundred. And among those volunteers were lawyers, doctors, clergymen, psychologists, dentists. They said, 'Look, we have money, but we need every dollar we have to keep up with the Joneses and live our lifestyles. But time we can give you.' I used to say, 'I don't want your money. I want something more important. I want you, I want your manpower.'"

Bonitas House also gets volunteer graduate students and unpaid interns from area colleges. Fr. Pat says the first job is to "knock off their conservative bourgeois edges. If somebody came in here with a Ph.D. from Harvard, my general response was, 'I won't hold it against you.'" There are 20 volunteers currently, and 5 full-time staff.

The summer of the fire, Fr. Pat and some of the boys were walking up 9th Street. "We were short a dime to buy a pizza for the boys. We figured we could hustle it on the way." One of the boys pointed out the FOR SALE sign on 606 East 9th Street and said, "'The heck with the pizza, Father. Why don't we buy the house?' We laughed all the way through the park."

Later, Fr. Pat decided maybe it was "a sign," and contacted the elderly lady who owned it. She told him "'I'll take 15 down.' I said, 'Oh, that's wonderful. I've got $20.' She said, 'Wait a minute, dear heart. I meant 15 *thousand*.'"

She later sold it to a partnership of investors—"an Irish guy, an Italian guy and a Jewish guy"—whom Fr. Pat proceeded to soften up. They offered it to him for $1,500 down, which a kindly donor provided, and a low fixed mortgage.

Moving his Puerto Rican and black kids onto the 600 block took some moxie. "Back in the 1960s, this block was lily white. No Hispanic or black could get further than Avenue C or D. It was Russian, Polish, German, Irish. You had the personification of insularity and bigotry combined. A protective bigotry. They weren't nasty, they were just protective of themselves."

Over the years, the house got renovated with donated materials and volunteer labor from construction workers and mechanics who trained the kids as apprentices. They furnished it with the refurbished furniture they'd found on the streets. It became a home for runaways, short-term or longer, and a halfway house for kids referred from the juvenile corrections system.

"I want to emphasize one point," Fr. Pat tells me. He says it slowly and proudly, stressing each word: "*We are not officially registered with any official government agency, and we refuse to do it*. We are living what we believe."

This attitude earned him some enemies among social workers and public-welfare types who questioned his credentials and his methods. "I fought the system," he says simply. He professes no patience for "ridiculous laws" and red-tape building codes. "Nobody wanted safety and security more than the occupants of the building . . . I didn't need to be told to protect us. But the city makes the demands so stringent that many many buildings that could be used today won't meet the code because the codes are unreasonable. Well, I defied every unreasonable code, and told them, 'Take me to court if you want.' They never did.

"You see," he continues, "I don't believe that you can't fight city hall. I believe that if city hall is wrong, you can fight them and beat them. I believe you can fight the Goliath of the federal government if you are a David with a pure heart."

By the '70s, the church was pushing him to complete his ordination into the priesthood. He responded with a typical maneuver. He met the local bishop of the Melkite Greek Catholic Church, which is separate from but affiliated with Roman Catholicism. Fr. Pat was clearly attracted to the way that Melkite parishes are more democratic than are Roman Catholic parishes; the Melkite priest is more a spiritual guide for his parishioners than "a monarchial priesthood, where he presides over his people. They'll tell him where to get off as quick as look at him."

He says, "It wasn't that I was disenchanted in any way" with the Roman Catholic Church. "I didn't run away from the West, I went to the East. There's an old expression, 'Out of the West came law. Out of the East came light.' I followed that light."

When the bishop "told me he'd approve" of his becoming a Melkite, "I said, 'I don't need your approval. You've God's approval and his blessing in our prosperity. But we're happy to become part of a larger entity so that our work can be perpetuated.'" He was ordained in 1977.

Then he pulled another rebellious move: he adopted an orphaned boy as his son. A Roman Catholic priest in Chicago had done it before, but permission was very rare. "I told the bishop I was going to do it, and he said, 'Do what you think best.' I'll tell you something about bishops, they'll sometimes say, 'Better you make a mistake than me getting involved.'" His son's now 21.

In the '80s, Fr. Pat says, the neighborhood began to see a "very large influx of aliens from all over the world—Ireland, Scotland, Italy, the [Caribbean] islands, Eastern Europe, Russia. These poor people lived in the woodwork." Fr. Pat began to work with these undocumented immigrants on both spiritual and temporal matters—"clandestinely," he points out, because "above all, anonymity is very important to them. But I want you to know, we never broke any law. We circumvented every law in the book. No law was ever broken. We found angles and loopholes."

"Unless you've lived among them," he continues, "unless you've known them, you can't know the fear, the anxiety, the terror that some of these people live in in this great land of the free. It's tragic." Fr. Pat recalls when the general amnesty for undocumented aliens was granted in '86. "I'll never forget the expression on the faces of my first 10 or 12 immigrants when they got their temporary work authorization. It was as if I'd given them a multimillion-dollar gift. They were ecstatic. People don't know the blessing of legality that we've got in this country." Since 1986, he estimates, he's helped up to 600 people get their green cards.

"I'm not a holy man," he says. "I don't pretend to be. I found a way of life that I'm very satisfied with, that's very rewarding for me, and I find that goodness is its own reward."

. . .

So that's Fr. Pat, feisty saint of Alphabet City. There's also Fr. Pat who was born and raised in Limerick and, though he became an American citizen, remains a proud son of Ireland.

"I don't apologize to anybody about my full support of the freedom fighters of occupied Ireland," he declares. "I never use the terms North and South. 'Occupied Ireland,' that's what it is, and until the occupiers leave, there'll never be peace." For freedom fighters, you might read the IRA.

"In the occupied parts of my country, there's still a war with England, which has 30,000 troops occupying it," Fr. Pat says. "I deplore any civilian violence. I want to be very clear on that point. There should never be a civilian target. But I quote—and I hate to quote the likes of him—Ronnie the rogue, former president of the United States, when challenged on what happened in Granada where 40 people were killed in a mental hospital, some of them children. Reagan's response was that there will necessarily be civilian casualties in war.

"Am I worked up about it? Yes I am. I'm an Irishman to the core. I am the son of an Irish freedom fighter who fought in 1916. A man who went to jail for four years . . . I'm my father's son and a son of Ireland as well. And, most importantly, I'm a citizen of the land of the free. I want for Ireland the freedom that this country has. There is no difference in my opinion between George Washington and the Minutemen of his time, and the freedom fighters of my country.

"I used to sit at the television and get so angry in my heart I wanted to take the nearest lamp and smash the tube. It was an ad for British Airways. This big fat Brit [actor Robert Morley] used to come on and say, 'Welcome home. All is forgiven.' How *dare* they? They pillaged and plundered and did for us, and we in America allow that type of ad? British imperialism is alive and well in America. I'll oppose it to my dying day—in Ireland *and* in America."

In 1982, "my brother and I had gone home to Ireland for our father's 87th birthday. We were having a family reunion." Meanwhile, culminating a couple years' investigation of suspected IRA gunrunners, the FBI was seizing an Ireland-bound shipment of goods on the waterfront in New Jersey. The goods were being shipped by his brother John, "an international shipper at the time of everything imaginable into Ireland from this country." The feds found an automatic rifle, some ammunition, electronic timing devices, and bulletproof vests, all packed under innocent goods.

Fr. Pat was seized in Ireland along with his brother, both charged with possession of contraband materials.

The case was tried in Dublin, in "special criminal court"—the "Diplock system" the British set up for dealing with suspected "freedom fighters" and supporters in Ireland, under which suspects could be held and interrogated without any charge being specified, prosecution witnesses did not have to appear; the case was heard by a tribunal of judges in closed court rather than before a jury.

"There's no way in the world that my brother John would ever have been convicted of any crime had he had a jury trial of his peers," Fr. Pat insists. Under the circumstances, "my brother took a plea. He had no choice." He was sentenced to 5 years in an Irish prison—which he served not as a common criminal, but as a political prisoner, with no parole and severe restrictions on visitors and other privileges.

Fr. Pat, meanwhile, was jailed "only for 5 days, but I was under house arrest in Ireland, constantly watched by their local Gestapo. I had to report each day between certain hours to the local police station. That went on from early June to the end of August." As the date set for his trial approached, the prosecution abruptly dropped all charges against him.

Fast-forward to November 12, 1993, and the FBI comes calling for the second time in his life.

"They came in and took me out in handcuffs. It was like a SWAT team. Almost like D-day, the invasion of Normandy, there were so many weapons out. And they didn't treat our youngsters very well, either. Put them up against the corridor wall with guns. A 70-year-old lady was standing in the hallway and they wouldn't allow her to sit down when she got weak. I was so flabbergasted—to say that I was shocked would be using a very mild term . . . I'd never seen anything as degrading and unjust."

Fr. Pat sat in M.C.C. from that Friday until his bail hearing on Tuesday. While he was in there, the feds, acting on an anonymous telephone tip, obtained a second search warrant to "re-raid this house. It was worse than World War II. They sealed off the entire block. They had a SWAT team, they had every imaginable artillery." They also raided his brother's next-door apartment.

"I am as innocent of these charges of being a Brinks robber as you are," Fr. Pat says, and I believe him. For all his flintiness, the image of this small, gray-haired priest trekking up to Rochester, donning a ski mask, and pulling an armed stickup is preposterous.

Strictly speaking, though, he's not charged with the robbery, but with being involved with the people who handled the cash afterward. This gets murkier. He says he never knew O'Connor, the Rochester inside man. Millar he did know, though he said "I never knew [him] under that name . . . Even though I'd baptized his children, I never knew his real name. We knew him by the name of Sam Campbell for about 5 years."

It's not unusual for illegal immigrants to use aliases, and in working with them, Fr. Pat says, "I don't ask too many questions . . . The undocumented don't trust anybody. Not even a clergyman. Not even their pastor. They only trust the seasoned."

But Fr. Pat admits he did know about "Sam Campbell's" past in Ireland. "Sam was arrested as a boy of 16. Interred as a juvenile, without trial, for alleged membership in a proscribed organization. Possibly meaning the IRA. He served his year and a half . . . He was the last man to get 'off the blanket' [i.e., the last prisoner to give up the strike] just before the death of Bobby Sands. He was in the prison block with Bobby Sands. He stood to the very last. I knew that. I revered the man because of who and what he was."

At the time of the arrests, it was widely reported in the media that during the months after the robbery Fr. Pat bought a brand-new Ford van with $26,000 in $20 bills. Calling this part of "the government's attempt to use trial by media to defame me," he declares that "I never even got behind the wheel of that vehicle, which indeed I did purchase, for a friend, with a $20,000 *loan* from National Westminster Bank . . . I have no reason to believe that our very efficient FBI wasn't fully aware of those facts when they made these allegations. That's the method the government uses."

Unfortunately for Fr. Pat's case, the friend he bought the van for was Sam Campbell / Millar. But Fr. Pat insists that it was done in all innocence—that he believed he was just helping out one of his families in need. "At the same time I co-signed a loan for a doctor who had gotten into bad credit, for a vehicle for $20,000. I told him, 'Hey, I'm already on one loan. I don't think they'll give it to you.'" Fr. Pat says that he's often helped people out that way, co-signing loans and mortgages and such, "and nobody ever betrayed me."

Then there's the 1st Avenue apartment that was raided. It "was an apartment used by various people, including ourselves," Fr. Pat concedes. "I've often subleased, or rented, or had the use of apartments in the greater community," to house overflow from Bonitas House as well as adults in need. "There's nothing at all unusual about us having the use of that apartment. And that is where money was found."

I ask, *So Fr. Pat, you never saw any of this money?* He responds, "I didn't say that. That's an area I couldn't go into. You'll have to talk to the lawyers. They wouldn't want me discussing it."

Okay. Let's assume Fr. Pat was aware that Millar was using the apartment to stash these bags of money. I ask him if maybe Millar was using *him* as well, taking advantage of Fr. Pat's sympathies and "reverence" for him.

"I can't imagine it," he replied. "I baptized three of his kids. He's not the type of man to use anybody. Not a bitter man. Raised his children in the church and so forth."

As for the IRA, Fr. Pat calls it "an organization with which I have nothing to do other than help families of ex-prisoners, and be sympathetic and totally outspoken and verbal for the cause of freedom and justice in the occupied part of my country."

Furthermore, he declares, "I am a total believer that the fruits of evil cannot be used for good . . . No way would I cooperate in or condone an action that would result in a crime. I am a crime *fighter*. The only Robin Hoodism I believe in is, if the landlord seizes your land, take it back. I will stretch it to say that if you're working for starvation wages in a bakery, and you can steal a loaf of bread and bring it home to feed your kids, I have no problem with that. But I would not approve of any people taking that which does not belong to them."

. . .

At the end of our two-hour session, Fr. Pat walks me to the door. He stands out on the front steps in the late afternoon sun, a small, gray-haired priest quietly returning greetings from just about everyone who walks by. He wears an unconscious frown as he surveys the street. He looks a little edgy and preoccupied—like a man trapped. There's that scrawl of graffiti across the way. *Free Fr. Pat.*

His lawyer has appealed for a change of venue from Rochester to New York. "It's not that I'm afraid of the people of Rochester. It's not that I don't feel there's a good judge up there, and a good prosecutor," Fr. Pat says. Rather, he argues that the expense of having to live in Rochester for the duration of a trial that could drag on for weeks is an unfair economic burden. He worries about who'll run things at the house while he's away.

At one point in our talk, he'd cited a few lines from the Book of Psalms. "Defend me, O God, and vindicate my cause from an unjust, ungodly nation. Protect me from the lying mouths of evil men." But then he paused and added that he couldn't believe the FBI were either evil or lying.

"I feel no ill will, anger or animosity against anybody," he said. "Not even the FBI and those people who arrested me . . . I respect the fact that the FBI must do their job, and should properly investigate. I deplore the way they do it. But I am hopeful and confident that when they realize that they've got the wrong person, they'll be big enough to recognize it."

Postscript

Later in 1994, Fr. Pat and Sam Millar were both convicted on the charge of possessing cash from the robbery. When I interviewed him he had neglected to mention some $168,000 in cash the FBI found in Bonitas House. Fr. Pat said he was holding it for illegal immigrant families who couldn't use a bank. The jury evidently did not believe him, even though none of the serial numbers on the bills matched any from the robbery.

Fr. Pat spent five years in a federal penitentiary in Pennsylvania. His adopted son, Jason, died while he was in there. Not allowed to come to New York for the funeral, which was held at Bonitas House, Fr. Pat conducted the service by telephone. (For more about Jason, see chapter 10 in this volume, on Baba Raul Canizares.)

The remaining $5 million from the heist has never been found.

Millar wrote a memoir about the heist, published in Ireland in 2003. There was talk of making a Hollywood movie based on it. Fr. Pat told the *New York Times* that the book was a work of "selective memory and poetic license," and cracked that Millar was "still trying to milk the cow he murdered long ago."

In November 2018, a few days after the Boston Irish gangster Whitey Bulger was beaten to death by fellow inmates in a maximum security prison in West Virginia, the *Irish Sun* reported that "Fr. Pat Maloney, 86, once described as 'the underground general of the IRA', claimed he has been asked to take part in the funeral of the notorious multi-murderer."

"I don't know the particular position of the church on a known criminal. But then the Lord is plentiful with redemption," Fr. Pat said. "In his own heart and soul, he may have changed. As far as I'm concerned, he'd be entitled to a Catholic burial."

Classic Fr. Pat.

As of 2021 he was still at Bonitas House, still being interviewed occasionally about the Brinks job, and still maintaining his innocence.

10 Baba Raul Canizares

Clayton and John

Where else but the Lower East Side would you find a practicing Cuban santero living under the same roof as a Melekite Irish Catholic priest? That's where Clayton met Baba Raul Canizares, when he lived and worked as a counselor at Bonitas House. Lionel's mystical Judaism, Fr. Pat's Eastern Catholicism, Baba Raul's Santeria—they're examples of how religion, mysticism, magic, witchcraft were all woven through the Lower East Side. And like most everything else cultural in the neighborhood, they often wove around one another and blended in unusual ways.

Clayton introduced John to Baba Raul in 1994, and John wrote this article for *NYPress*.

. . .

Raul Canizares is a very large physical presence. Think of Paul Prudhomme with a Cuban accent, wearing a loose, embroidered West African outfit. He also projects a larger personal presence, warm and friendly, but with some deep core of composure that seems to center him, a dignified self-assurance that you'd want to call grace, in both senses of the word.

For all that, you might not instantly picture him with an M.A. in religious studies, going for his Ph.D. in anthropology, teaching two university courses as an adjunct professor, and writing a treatise on the Yoruban roots of Cuban Santeria (*Walking with the Night*, Destiny Books, 1993). You might more easily picture him actually officiating at a candle-lit Santeria altar, the shadows wild with drums and chants and incense, ritually slitting the throat of a chicken and offering its blood to one of the Santeria saints.

In fact he's both a scholar of Santeria, teaching "the first full course in Santeria in a major theological school" at the University of South Florida, and a fully initiated santero (priest), which he says he was predestined in the womb to become. Born in Havana, he comes from a long line of santeria and santeros on his mother's side. He was initiated as a santero at the age of seven. Now, as Santeria spreads in the U.S., he's become a spokesman and interlocutor for a way of worship most often characterized by its secretiveness and aura of mystery.

In a way, Canizares's double life is emblematic of Santeria in general. Santeria's roots are in the Yoruban culture of West Africa. Brought to Cuba as slaves, where they became known as Lucumi, Yorubans carried their religion with them. Over the years it got mixed up with the dominant Cuban Catholicism, much like the way Candomble developed in Brazil, and Vodun/Voodoo developed in Haiti and New Orleans.

In Santeria, everything flows from a first principle and creating force, Ashé. Canizares explains that contrary to most Western theology, with its dualisms of good and evil, right and wrong, the concept of Ashé is more like Hindu and Buddhist concepts of dharma and karma. Ashé is the force of cosmic balance; you can either be in harmony with it or in discord. The harmonious life reaps karmic rewards, while bad luck, illness, and unhappiness are the signs of a life out of balance.

Santeria posits a supreme being with two aspects, Olodumare and Olofi. "In the beginning was Ashé," Canizares writes, "and Ashé was everything. When Ashé began to think, Ashé became Olodumare. When Olodumare began to act, Olodumare became Olofi . . ."

Olodumare / Olofi dwells alone, remote and removed from the world of men. A pantheon of lesser divine beings, the orishas, are the agents who operate between that realm and ours, interceding in ways something like the saints of popular Catholicism.

The two most powerful orishas are Obatala, the head orisha, and Eleggua, lord of the crossroads and messenger between the gods and men. Other very powerful orishas are Shango, lord of drumming and music; Yemaya, queen of the sea; Oshun, queen of rivers; Ogun, lord of iron and war; and Oya, lord of storms and cemeteries. There are various lesser orishas as well—about a dozen in all, Canizares says, who are popular with believers.

As in Vodun and Voodoo, believers in Santeria have very direct, physical contact with the orishas. Dedicated participants are the "children" of specific orishas, who take a parental interest in their lives. As Santeria ceremonies, the orishas are called on with drums and chanting, offers of rum and cigars and food. The orishas literally "possess" the faithful, in ways very similar to the loas of Vodun and Voodoo taking over the bodies of their human "horses." Fantastic changes are said to come over them: voice and posture are altered, they may display extraordinary strength or knowledge, and so on. To outsiders, it can look like the demonic possessions of Catholicism.

"It doesn't happen too often in front of profane eyes," Canizares smiles when I mention this. "But you're right. The term possession has a very negative connotation in American culture, while the term possession in Santeria has a divine connotation. In America, you think Linda Blair and split pea soup coming out of her mouth. But when you say *possessed* in the context of Santeria, you think of communion with God—or one aspect of God, aspects of divine light."

As a lifelong santero, Canizares says he has been possessed by the orishas many times. I ask him what it feels like.

"This is how it feels. You begin to lose consciousness, but very slowly. And then, like at a psychedelic movie, you begin to see things shifting around. And then all of a sudden you black out. And then you come to, and you feel very relaxed, very lighthearted. And people tell you that you were possessed, but you don't remember anything that happened. The term 'mounted' is used, because you're like a horse and they ride you.

"What happens is, your ego fights with them, and that's why you see all this strange psychedelic stuff. Your ego is trying not to leave, and they're trying to enter, and then—*oof*." He makes a shoving gesture with both hands. "They push your ego aside. Your ego is . . . the analogy would be *asleep*. You're in a very deep sleep, and you're not sure how many hours have elapsed. When you come to, the time is only like a second for you, but the orisha could have been talking through your for 3 or 4 hours."

That's the usual time span, but "the longest on record is 9 days. That was a scary thing. It's famous in Cuba. It was a man who made fun of his orisha. His orisha took him over and said, 'I'm not leaving you. You made fun of me, I'm going to be here forever.' Finally they appeased the orisha with offerings and promises what he would never do it again."

I ask him if the orishas are personalities with specific identities.

"Oh, definitely. They're archetypes. They're almost exaggerated in their attributes. For example, Shango is virile, beautiful, macho. But he is also very eclectic, in that to get out of bad situations he dresses up as a woman. Yemaya is the nurturing mother. She's very serious, very loving, very stately. Oshun has different aspects, but in the most popular she's called the divine whore. She has a bod on her, and she likes to show it off. Some people call her the African Aphrodite. Or maybe Aphrodite is the Greek Oshun. We'll have to see which one is right," he grins, referring to the controversy over whether ancient culture spread from central Africa north into Egypt and Greece. At any rate, "Oshun is definitely an Aphrodite or Venus-like character."

In Cuba, Santeria was always the religion of the poor, mostly black, and looked down on, if not actively repressed, by the Hispanic Catholic upper classes (although, as Canizares points out, many of them secretly participated). To survive, Santeria enthusiastically borrowed many Catholic trappings—there are Santeria "masses," and many of the orishas are closely identified with Catholic saints. While dedicated Santeria practitioners know the difference, Canizares says, more casual participants often believe that they're simply practicing Catholicism.

Because of this mixing, academics have considered Santeria a syncretic religion, meaning, in Canizares's interpretation, an "unconscious, uncritical adoption of the dominant culture's religious beliefs." Canizares disagrees. The Catholic trappings, he argues, are really clever dissimulation, a screen of accepted images and icons behind which Afro-Cubans were allowed to practice their beliefs without being hassled.

It's not very different, he contends, from the pagans in early medieval Europe who were able to keep their gods and practices alive by disguising them as Catholic saints and rites. So Saint Bridget was the Catholicized version of a Celtic goddess, the cult of the Virgin had aspects of earlier cults of Diana, and Christmas is a thinly disguised pre-Christian festival. Ismaili Muslims practiced similar deceptions to hide their true beliefs from the more powerful Sunni.

"It's amazing," he says to me, "how the Church officially condemns Santeria for being allegedly syncretistic, when the Catholic Church itself is the most syncretistic body on earth."

Canizares insists that Yorubans in Cuba consciously seized on similarities between their beliefs and popular Cuban Catholicism, which, with its wealth of saints and variations on Jesus and Mary—not to mention its own brands of "superstition" and "magic"—provided great cover. Shango, the king who traditionally wears red, becomes Saint Barbara, the patron saint of soldiers, traditionally depicted wearing a crown and a red cloak. Babalu Aye, the orisha who rules over smallpox, was associated with the leper Lazarus. Obatala wears the outer appearance of the Catholics' Our Lady of Mercy, Oshun takes on the guise of Our Lady of Charity, and so on.

Casual participants include people who occasionally or habitually consult Santeria practitioners for counseling "much as they would use the services of a psychologist or a physician." They may seek herbal remedies for health problems, magic potions to help with their love life, or ask the orishas for advice about the future. Many prominent Cubans "would not make a move without first consulting with their santero," Canizares says. Until quite recently, such casual participants were often unaware that they were praying to African gods, not Catholic saints. And if asked, most santeros would tell you they were Catholics.

"From a santero's perspective," Canizares writes, "it is not wrong to celebrate a feast to the orishas on Saturday night and go to mass Sunday morning. Many santeros have developed a genuine affection for Catholic saints and enjoy mass for the same reasons other Catholics do . . . However, knowledgeable santeros are perfectly aware of the differences between the orishas and the saints." And, he says to me, "aware of its Africanness, and its distinctiveness from any Western Judeo-Christian or Islamic tradition."

Canizares's own legacy is quite remarkable. He lists his background as "Spanish-Yoruban-French-Italian-Canary Islander-Filipino-Native American." His father's family was aristocratic and European, his mother's more humble and racially mixed.

Oddly, his father's legitimate grandfather may have been his mother's illegitimate great-grandfather: Count Brunet, a wealthy landowner in the Cuban town of Trinidad. In 1870, his mother's grandmother, a servant in Brunet's household, gave birth to a dark-skinned, red-haired son, who had a purple birthmark on his tongue in the shape of a double-edged ax—a sign of Shango. Also, he was born on December 4, a day associated with Shango. So, though officially named Jose, he was called Bangoche, a name given to Shango's chosen. Later he became a famous curandero (fortune-teller and he healer), and Count Brunet deeded him a small piece of land.

As a curandero, Bangoche got into conflict with Andrea Ortiz, a white woman who was the most powerful bruja (witch) in Trinidad. Ortiz was so feared that her own granddaughter, also named Andrea Ortiz, changed her name to Ophelia. ("To her," Canizares tells me, having her terrifying grandmother's name "was almost like being named Satan.") Bangoche and Ortiz settled their differences by becoming lovers, producing four offspring, including Canizares's grandmother Juana.

Juana's daughter Ana Rosa became a famous Cuban stage and film star under the name Roxana Gonzales. As a much sought-after star, she would eventually enter marriages with three wealthy men—a Jewish-Canadian millionaire, a famous Mexican entertainer, and Raul Canizares-Verson, the Count Brunet, Canizares's father.

Santeria being looked down upon in Cuban high society, she kept secret from them for 40 years the fact that she was a priestess of Shango. She dedicated her son to become a priest of Obatala before he was born; by the time he was seven he had gone through most of the initiations of a santero. As he was growing up in the '50s and early '60s, his family did a lot of traveling back and forth between Havana and Brooklyn. By the late '60s they were no longer allowed back into Cuba. "I still consider Brooklyn very much a spiritual home for me," he says.

Canizares remembers that when he was a boy the family chauffeur drove him and his mother to an important Santeria feast, a bembé. They drove from El Vedado—the "forbidden zone" of Havana, where wealthy, mostly white people lived—to the poor black outskirts. He writes: "As the big, black Buick left behind the sterile paved boulevards of El Vedado and entered the blood-red mud pathways of Mantilla, a change came over its three occupants. No longer was Andres the part-time chauffeur taking his rich employer and her little boy out for a drive; he became an elder santero who was guiding his young sister in religion and her son . . ."

At the bembé, his mother "looked quite different from the white lady she seemed to be a few minutes before. It was as if her African heritage, hidden under her father's European skin, had emerged from some recondite spot within her where it had lain dormant, waiting to be called."

As in other religions, there's a hierarchy to the Santeria priesthood. To become a santero or santera requires a ceremony called the "kariocha," from the Lucumi for "to seat on the head." The ceremony includes shaving the head and making a small incision in the scalp into which an orisha's secret, paste like substance is placed; the orisha's power is thus instilled in the recipient. Only the seven most powerful orishas are "seated."

The ceremony comes after usually three years of study in Cuba, though that's been reduced in the faster-paced States. During that time the initiate learns to make magic potions and herbal concoctions, how to divine the future from cowrie shells, and how to speak at least the liturgical uses of ancient Lucumi language. Some santeros are chosen by the orishas to go on to become babalaos, the "high priests" of Santeria.

Although outsiders have penetrated some distance into the private world of Santeria and described some of the rituals, it remains a very secretive way of life, both by tradition and, Canizares would argue, necessity. He says that when word got out among santeros that he was writing an insider's book, he got some "almost threatening letters."

Yet in *Walking with the Night*, while he offers plenty of historical and theological insights, he preserves the secrecy of the ceremonies and practices. And when I ask if he's a practicing santero now, he gives me an amused and sly smile. "That's an interesting question. If I told you no, I could be very well dissimulating. Whatever I answer, the knowledgeable people will have trouble with it."

In the U.S., Santeria would have remained of interest only to religious scholars and ethnographer were it not for its growing and controversial presence here over the last decade. Canizares outlines the history for me.

"According to my research, the first santeros came to the United States in the late 19th century, to work in the cigar factories of Key West and Tampa. But the first major incursion of the religion in the United States was in 1946, here in New York," when a Cuban-born immigrant, Pancho Mora, attempted to organize santeros in the Bronx. "It was mostly a Puerto Rican and Cuban thing until the 1960s, when it became very much a black thing."

It was then that the man formerly known as Walter King went to Nigeria, the seat of Yoruban culture, where the "emperor" Oni of Ife—a traditional Yoruban title without political portfolio but greatly respected in Nigeria—named him a Yoruban oba, or "king." There are 60 such obas, but until Walter King—renamed Osejiman Adefumi I—they were all in Nigeria. As Asdefumi, King became an important figure in the black power movement of the 1960s. He stressed the African nature of Santeria, de-emphasizing the Catholic veneer and the Cuban connection. Today, Adefumi runs a back-to-the-roots Yoruban cultural center called Oyotunji Village in South Carolina.

In the '80s and '90s, Santeria's presence here has greatly increased with the growth in Cuban, Puerto Rican, and other Latin American communities. Canizares says hard figures on the numbers of participants here are difficult to come by "because it's still a largely secret religion for many people." New York City is generally considered "second in the nation in the amount of santeros. Judging by the botanicas and some of the best guesstimates, a conservative number would be 500,000. However, there are different degrees of participation. Out of those 500,000, I would say probably 45,000 are hardcore, full-time, totally devoted santeros." In Miami there are about 60,000 full-time santeros, he estimates, but when you add "the people who just go to a santero for help, the number goes up to a million, easy."

As Santeria became more visible in the 1980s, animal rights activists, including the Humane Society, began to protest its most visible aspect: the practice of animal sacrifice. The orishas expect direct propitiations and offerings from their faithful, including offerings of food. Animals are ritually slain, their throats slit and the blood collected to be poured over objects sacred to the orishas.

The carcasses are sometimes cooked and eaten, but more traditionally they must be disposed of at special symbolic sites dictated by the orishas—at crossroads, cemeteries, by railroad tracks or a riverbank. Failure to do it right negates the purpose of the offering.

Animal sacrifice has caused some of Santeria's worst publicity in the U.S. Newspapers carry gruesome stories of bloody animal parts gathering flies on street corners, attracting rats to basements or floating into community water supplies.

In south Florida, neighbors of a Santeria church in Hialeah put together a petition in 1987 and got the city to pass a bunch of laws outlawing the practice. The church took the city to court, arguing that its First Amendment rights to religious expression were being violated. The dispute reached the Supreme Court in '92. The high court had previously upheld bans on Mormon polygamy and Southern snake handling; just two years earlier, it had upheld the ban against Native Americans' use of peyote as a religious sacrament. So it was a surprise move when it overturned the Hialeah ban last year.

Canizares applauds that decision, but he's only cautiously optimistic about its real effect in the ongoing clash of cultures. He contends that it's hypocritical for a meat-eating, Chicken McNuggets culture like ours to object to the slaying of a few hens.

"When people say they think that animal sacrifice is barbaric, they're actually saying, 'It's barbaric they're not worshipping God the same way we are,'" he says. "This was such a blatant attack on a religion. In Hialeah, you can kill animals for sport, you can kill an animal for food, you can kill an animal for humane reasons, but you cannot kill it for Santeria. So it was specifically aimed at that.

"Interestingly enough, the mayor of Hialeah was a believer," he adds, who went along with the legislation to placate voters. A few months later, a babaloa confronted the mayor on tv, "and a few weeks later he was indicted for bribery, and served some time in jail." Canizares smiles and shrugs.

He knows it might be more acceptable if the slain animal were cooked and eaten after the ceremony. He says that in fact when larger animals are sacrificed—pigs, goats, rams—they usually are then cooked and eaten. It's the smaller ones, mostly chickens and pigeons, that aren't.

Still, because four-footed animals are only sacrifice for major ceremonies, and the birds are used far more often, the problem of disposition of the carcasses will remain a point of contention, even considering the Supreme Court ruling. In Florida, Canizares had proposed creating "a kind of miniature Santeria Disneyland, where there would be like a little crossroads, a little mountain," and other simulated sites symbolic to the orishas. "American know-how, right?" he laughs.

And santeros would use it?

"Yes. Santeros are very adaptable. For example, in some of their rituals, santeros are supposed to bathe in a river. Well, suppose they're in New York in December. They do it in the bathtub. And it's perfectly okay."

Then again, he predicts, "Santeria is going to have to come to a decision. What I suspect will happen is a branch of Santeria will give up animal sacrifice, and it will become something else. The purists will maintain the use of animal sacrifice, and they shall be the minority."

. . .

Santeria's loose associations with the sinister Latin American tradition of Palo Mayombe don't help its image. With its roots in another African culture altogether, Palo is more black witchcraft than religion, a system of magical spells and unsavory practices, including human sacrifice, used to gain power and harm enemies. Manuel Noriega is a practicing Palermo, as were the Matamoros mass murderers.

Santeria is often confused with Palo, especially among conservative Christian types who believe we're under siege from an international Satanic cult of child-stealing ritual killers. And Canizares admits that believers in Santeria aren't above turning to paleros when they want a trabajo (spell) worked on an enemy. As one old santero once said to him, "Getting results with Santeria is almost as slow as getting results with the [Catholic] Church; you ask your saint for things and you wait for him to help you . . . If you want to feel good, you worship the orishas. If you want something done, you go to a palero."

"Palo is adamantly 'We'll do whatever we need to do,'" Canizares says. "Palo does not have any problems with saying, 'If somebody tries to mess with me, I'll fuck them up.' It's a frightening thing—the use of magic with no moral consequence, no ethical concerns. When a santero wants something bad done, they don't go to another santero, they go to a palero. That's where the two meet. But according to Santeria, they will encounter the karmic consequence if they choose to do that. Palo is definitely a weapon that does not judge who it strikes. But in Santeria, if you go to the orisha and say, 'So and so was mean to me, I want him dead,' the orisha will say, 'Well, he was mean to you, but maybe you deserve that. What he did was not bad enough for you to want to kill him.' But in Palo they go, 'Okay.' *Poof.*"

Canizares says that he's personally seen one Palo spell "worked right in front of me. And the person to whom it was done did die. However, that could have been a coincidence."

I offer the pop-psychology explanation that if the person on whom the spell was cast believes in it enough, it could kill him.

Canizares gives me a crooked smile. "I think that's an old white folks' tale," he says bluntly. "The person in this case did not know about the spell. This person had no idea that the spell was on him. That's scarier, right?" He laughs. "I do believe, however—because this person was not a religious person—that if a person has a strong spirituality, spells can't touch him. Whether it's Hare Krishna or Catholic or Jewish or whatever, I have never seen people of real spirituality be affected by spells. So maybe it's the other way around. Maybe it's people who *don't* believe, who don't have strong anchors in the spirituality of the earth, maybe those are the people who get swept away."

Another reason for Santeria's increased visibility recently is that it's been attracting white intellectuals. Not surprisingly, Canizares says they often come to it from Wicca and other New Age fads.

To Canizares, the new influx of white practitioners "is the most fascinating part of my latest research. In Tampa, there are, that I know of, six major centers of Anglo santeros."

Where black Americans say they're attracted to Santeria as a way of exploring their roots, "white people give totally different answers. Of course," he grins, "they wouldn't be saying to discover their roots. The white people say 'It gives me an edge in the rat race.'"

He cites a Tampa professor he knew "who wanted a tenured position she was not qualified for." When someone else got the job, she cast a spell on him. Which sounds like black magic to me, but Canizares had a typically innocent-sounding answer. "It worked out very well. He got offered and Ivy League position, so he left, and she got the Tampa position."

Canizares believes one of the main attractions for new converts is the physicality of Santeria, the sensuality of it. "Aesthetically, it's a very beautiful tradition. Also, the idea of worship is very different from the Western sense. For this, worship is sweating and dancing. If you get sexually excited, it's okay. It's part of the whole thing. It's not lewdness, but there is that earthiness to it.

"It's a religion that you experience with all your senses," he goes on. "And because you experience it with all your senses, it's thought that the only place for this information to go is to the soul . . . You have the smell which is the incense. You have the taste, which is the rum. You have the air, which is the cigar. You have the touch, which is the drumming and dancing. You have the sight, which is the beads and the color."

When I spoke to Canizares he'd just come back from Cuba—the traveling's much easier than it was 20 years ago. Interestingly, he's found that Santeria is undergoing an intellectuals' renaissance there, too, with Castro's blessing.

"In the beginning, Castro tried to stamp it out as one of the many religions," he recalls. "Then he discovered that his base of support was mainly black Cuba. And black Cuba would not stand for him deriding their deep spirituality. So he made a complete turnaround." Santeria was officially recognized first as an important folklore, "and now he's openly praising it as a true expression of the people."

In fact, I note, I'd heard that Castro was a practicing santero himself.

"Yes. I know for a fact that he's into Palo, and I have anecdotal evidence that he's also probably a santero. But it may also be that he leaks that so that practitioners look at him with a certain amount of empathy."

With Castro's support, Santeria is no longer socially unacceptable in Havana. "And it has become much more intellectual. In the '50s and '60s, most of the practitioners were black people of the lower class, who barely had a grammar school education. Today, the religion is barely being practiced by university professors, physicians . . . At a bembé last week, I met a Cuban babalao. I was amazed at the amount of erudition. This man was an exquisite conversationalist. Whereas in the old days the babalaos could hardly speak Spanish. They spoke what we call Bozal, a mixture of African and Spanish.

"There's a lot of contact between Nigeria and Cuba. The emperor visited Cuba with full state honors. As we're speaking, he's looking to name a king in Cuba, which has never happened before. So it has acquired a tremendous amount of cachet. My book, by the way," Canizares smiles, "is being pirated in Cuba very successfully. I don't mind at all."

There's a funny side to this. In international Santeria circles, there's a still a tradition that the best santero initiations are the ones done in Cuba.

And—much like other rites of passage ceremonies, including the first "first holy communion" in some Catholic cultures or weddings in most all cultures—the kariocha can be an extremely expensive event, something the initiates and their families can spend their life savings on.

Castro has picked up on this as a way of bringing hard foreign currency in. You can be made a santero in Cuba for $3,000—"which is a bargain," Canizares says, by standards in the U.S, where depending on how elaborate the ceremony is, the cost can be $5,000 to a daunting $50,000.

"People say, 'Why is this so expensive?'" Canizares says. "But it's very involved. The intricacy of the ceremony, the materials, and the people of high degree of training that you need. It's mind-boggling. You have to pay those persons."

Which brings up another example of American know-how being applied to Santeria. Canizares cites "a *very* controversial man, Philip John Niemark, in Chicago. He became a babalao man, Philip John Niemark, in Chicago. He became a babalao in Africa. He came back and allegedly is making a lot of his fellow Jews santeros. He was a millionaire stock broker. He's organizing initiators like 'Bring a friend and get 50 percent off.'"

Canizares laughs. "That's the word on him in the Santeria community. I think there may be an element of jealousy, because he's being very successful in attracting people to be initiated. Money is a tremendous concern. I know a lot of people who want to become santeros but don't have the money for the initiation. Now this man says, 'Make a party of 10, we'll give you a *real* big discount.' So you have chartered bus loads of people coming to him.

"Some of the purists think this is not religion he's practicing, it's more like mass marketing. I don't know. I do know that he went over to Africa and received the blessing of the emperor, which made a lot of African-Americans astounded. It makes him a very bona fide santero."

And that reminds me of another kind of bona fides: as the son of the late Count Brunet, I ask, has Canizares claimed the title for himself?

"Officially, I've never done anything about it," he replies. "I had a letter saying the title is vacant unless I do something about it. I haven't decided yet. I've always been pretty radical, ultra-leftist. To be a count . . . ?"

Then he shrugs and grins. "But in my old age, I'm beginning to think that it might be fun," he says with true Santeria equanimity. "What the hell?"

Postscript

Baba Raul was a renaissance man. He was the academic expert on world religions and author of several books on Santeria and Palo. But he was also the practicing santero, deep into the mystical, intuitive aspects of it. He held a number of Santeria seances at Clayton Gallery, in which he went into trances and was entered by Shango. He used the Obi method of casting a handful of coconut shell fragments to tell fortunes. He was fascinated with Lady Armida, owner of the Wiccan store Lady and the Moon in a basement on St. Mark's Place.

He was also an artist, who painted and sculpted Elegguas. Most people who want an Eleggua statue for their home go to the botanica and buy one, but Baba sculpted a personalized one for you. He depicted your spiritual self as he saw it; the resulting figure could be pretty bizarre. He sculpted around a cardboard toilet paper roll, and then it was your task to collect the various elements that would get sealed in there. Water from a river, water from an ocean, dirt from a crossroads, dirt from in front of a bank, something silver, something gold, like that. When it was sealed, he would sacrifice a chicken, and blow cigar smoke and rum on the statue, and that brought Eleggua to life. He made one for Clayton.

Genesis P-Orridge, the musical and psychosexual experimenter who moved to New York in the early 1990s from England, spent a year studying with Baba. And then there was Jason Patino, the young man Fr. Pat adopted. Fr. Pat has always done good works for people, but he does them in his own way. You ask a typical priest for help and he'll pray for you. Fr. Pat makes things happen. He knew Jason's mother. She was shot in the back in the Bronx, and asked Fr. Pat on her deathbed to take care of her son. So Fr. Pat adopted him.

Jason became fascinated with Santeria and devoted to Raul as his padrino, his godfather and mentor. Fr. Pat was not pleased at all. After a while, Raul wasn't either, because Jason began exploring Palo, the dark side of Santeria. Jason was a nice kid, a good kid; anyone could see he wasn't equipped to deal with the dark side. Raul begged him to stop. Jason started hanging around bad crowds uptown, apparently involved in heavy drugs or something else criminal, and was brutally murdered.

Baba died in 2002. He had just turned 47. Clayton held a celebration of his life at the gallery, followed by a seance.

11 Jim Power

Clayton

In 2020, despite the pandemic, 73-year-old Jim Power was still out on the streets of the East Village, still working on his mosaics that decorate neighborhood light poles and stop lights, curbs, shops, bars, and restaurants. He'd been doing it since in 1985.

Clayton wrote this about him in *The Villager* in March 2012.

. . .

One lesson I learned from living on the Lower East Side is that there is no heaven on earth, no utopia, no perfect solution to all of life's problems, which means life is about dealing with the good and the bad, the ugly and the beautiful, the rational and the insane. And one of the major blessings of the old Lower East Side was it had a full mixture of every combination of opposites. Then add in the stimulus of the multiple layers of ethnic culture that each immigrant group left behind. Then there was what seemed like an endless variety of highly charged creative activity going on—dance, performance, poetry, film, painting, music, politics, sex, drugs, lifestyles—that coexisted with and inspired those around them. Yes, the old Lower East Side had its problems, but it was a place where you felt you had the chance to follow your dreams, or nightmares, whichever.

It was rich in distinctive, one-of-a-kind characters. Jim Power is one of the last such characters. I have known and documented Jim for more than a couple of decades. Jim is a complicated individual with a complex personality that can go through as many changes as the pea in a shell game. He is one of the only people who can make me laugh till my eyes tear up, or so angry I never want to see him again. He has a tremendous capacity for love, kindness, and empathy for those who are struggling, or are helping him, or are his friends. Yet, on another day, to the same people, he can be ruthlessly vile, mean, and hurtful.

I have witnessed him angry to the point of insanity, screaming in the middle of the street, because of some perceived injustice, or to teach us a lesson. Jim once caught Phil Hartman, creator of the HOWL Festival and FEVA, in what he felt was a lie, which drove Jim crazy to the point of using his claw hammer to smash his Avenue A Veterans of Foreign Wars mosaic. Jim was a veteran of a foreign war and he hated Phil's lie. As the HOWL parade came down Avenue A Jim attacked the pole. At the same time, an elderly Polish man was pleading, "Jim, no! Jim, no!" What shocked me most about this moment was this was one of the first times, outside of business, when an old-school Polish neighbor protested anything outside of his own community!

Jim is one of the most opinionated, stubborn, over-the-top, egotistical, narcissistic, bigger-than-life, old-school individuals you are likely to ever run into.

Yes, Jim is a character. But what makes him special is his dedication to community and his art. Though not obligated to enlist, he joined the army and went to fight in Vietnam. In some ways, Jim has never left the war. The war is here. The war is now. He is living it, and fighting it.

His first-generation Irish family was in good standing in the carpenters union. Jim joined the union and learned the trade. Union job, good pay, excellent benefits. He gave it all up to follow his dream of beautifying the Lower East Side—a dream he has paid a high price to follow.

Jim has spent most of his adult life living close to the bottom tier of society. He was almost a squatter, but was too right-wing for his anarchist roommates. Every place he lived with other people turned into a disaster. Small basement spaces and furnace rooms seem to suit him best. He almost never paid rent, but he always worked and made some money. He lives by his wits. Jim is a survivor, but living a spartan life for sure.

The early years were the hardest. The streets he worked on were dangerous. He was making art against all odds. A heroic effort, no question.

His mosaic street art is one of the few constants that has not been destroyed or wiped out by gentrification or NYU or Cooper Union, though there have been attempts. The impact of gentrification can be almost overwhelming—watching the destruction of the very roots of a neighborhood, its character, its history. His mosaics are a stabilizing factor that make some people feel safer.

I've heard people say that after they come up the subway stairs at Astor Place, they feel like they're home when they see Jim's decorated lampposts.

I'm not sure why his poles act as a deterrent to crime. Maybe it's the brightness, the glitter, the enshrined people who cross all color lines, the salute to the workers—the Fire Department, Sanitation, the Police Department—or the historic locations, like the Fillmore pole with famous acts who played there. But for whatever reason—respect, maybe—there is less criminal activity around his poles. Those of us from the old school are all familiar with the criminal activity around street corners.

Jim's mosaics are probably the most photographed public sculpture in New York City. Hang out by the Cube on Astor Place and see how many people take pictures of his work. Neighborhood kids grew up with those mosaics; some helped put in a piece of broken tile when they were, let's say, 11, with their mother standing there. Then, by chance, 12 years later, the person sees Jim working: the connection is deep, as the synapses instantly snap back to an inspired, unique moment, a visual and tactile memory of participating in making historic art.

His work has changed over the years, although there's always a connection to smashed dishes and ceramics. Compare the light poles on 3rd Avenue and St. Mark's. The early ones were crudely made, with massive pieces of broken pottery. But they're still out there, surviving under the worst of NYC conditions, from storms to dogs to bicycle chains. Jim's work has lasted.

Many of the mosaics work on multiple levels. There is the identifiable distant image, like the full-size American flag on the lamppost at St. Mark's and 2nd Avenue. Take a close look and you'll see stories within stories. There's his salute-to-Yiddish-theater pole, sporting the names of famed venues, such as the Commodore, the Anderson, the Eden, and Minsky's Burlesque, as well as performers, from Molly Picon to the Bowery Boys, to Burns and Allen, to Bob Hope celebrating his 100th birthday. In Power's creative vision, Hope connects back to the U.S.O., to a mention of M.I.A. P.O.W. and "American Theater of War," to the small writing on the bottom of a teacup that reads "Salute to U.S. Armed Forces."

The public work—the lampposts, the planters—Jim does at his own expense. To survive, he takes on paying jobs. He has done Pie Studios, where the Rolling Stones love his work; signs for tattoo parlors in Sicily; kitchen cabinets in people's homes; a mosaic shield for a retiring police chief.

He always feels underappreciated, disrespected, ignored, disregarded. Jim has never quit working or given up on his dream of beautifying the LES. He has led one of the most dedicated and difficult art-life struggles of anyone I know. Jim is a true warrior of the highest honor.

Jim's mosaics define the East Village. They make the place home.

12 Cochise

Clayton

I first met Cochise in 1992. One day there was a constant and aggressive ringing of my doorbell. Standing there were three menacing-looking guys, all wearing gang colors, black and red, in a design that looked like the embroidered patches a motorcycle club wears on the back of their jackets. The top rocker in black letters with a red background read, "SATAN'S SINNERS." On the bottom rocker, in the same color scheme, was "NOMADS." The middle patch was made of a white skull with a red eye patch covering the left eye, wearing a WWII German black helmet with a red swastika in the middle. The background had an outline of flame in black. A strong image, to say the least.

From the person I assumed was the leader I got the intimidating: "Yo, what's up?" Followed by, "I hear that you've been documenting people in the park and giving the information to the cops." Meaning Tompkins Square Park, where I shot a lot of photos and video. A young squatter punk woman who had fallen for one of the Sinners had fed him lies that I, a person who was constantly photographing and filming the park conflicts with the cops in my attempt to document the scene, was really a police stooge who was giving copies of my tapes and photos to them.

Slowly and cautiously we went through the false charges. I explained the consequences I am still dealing with stemming from my 1988 police riot tapes. Those tapes, which exposed out-of-hand police roughing up civilians, had dire consequences for the boys in blue, as I explained. Based on my tapes, cops were fired, six cops criminally indicted, and a captain moved out of precinct. Then I explained my court cases, my arrests, the warrants on me, subpoenas, and so on. Cochise was intelligent and wise enough not to prejudge me based on rumors, but to listen carefully to what I had to say. As I talked, he came to the understanding that, for whatever unfathomable reason, I was being set up.

I discovered that the Satan's Sinners had no connection to motorcycles, but were a street gang. Actually, they were the last of the classic

Lower East Side street gangs to wear traditional gang colors and jackets. They started when Cochise got out of prison in 1988. The members I got to know were: Heavy, Manny, Mantis, Spider, Rocco, Jose, Pyro, Homicide, Tito, Chaos, Ed, Angel (Squirt), Mudo, China, Donna, Marian, and Black Widow. As you can guess from this lineup, the Sinners, unlike most gangs, had women as full members. Some of the women were hardcore gang-bangers and others just liked the sense of family.

Their clubhouse was in a casita (a small shack), in a lot between 3rd Street and 4th Street from Avenue C to D. Casitas were used to store garden equipment and supplies, and acted as summer kitchens and sheltered hangouts.

I became friends with Cochise, whose given name is Jose Quiles, which meant that I was able to document the Sinners. I was given unlimited access. And in return, I did what I could to help them with whatever useful assets I could provide. After I learned that Cochise was the person who designed the club's colors, I knew that he was an authentic artist, so I persuaded him to get involved with painting and drawing. He produced a sizable body of artwork and I included him in some art shows in my gallery. I was able to persuade Bert Waide Hemphill Jr. to come look at Cochise's work. Bert was one of the founding members of the American Folk Art Museum. One day Bert and I came to visit Cochise at the clubhouse, and Bert purchased some of Cochise's work. When Bert passed, his collection ended up in museums.

Since the Sinners were the last street gang wearing the colors on the Lower East Side, and the neighborhood's gangs have been so overlooked, I wanted to get them as much exposure as possible. I got a few of the members—including Heavy, Mantis, Manny, and Cochise—on the late Flo Kennedy's cable show and some local news programs, and arranged for a few articles and interviews in newspapers and magazines.

The gang was interested in tattoos. Most of the tattoos they had were done by hand poking. Cochise and Heavy wanted professional tattoos done with modern electric equipment. Since I was the president of the Tattoo Society of New York, I brought them to a club meeting and introduced them to artists. This was during a period when tattoos were illegal in the city, and it was an underground activity. One of the top artists (Sean Vasquez) did Satan's Sinner tattoos for Cochise and Heavy. Cochise in turn gave me a handmade prison tattoo machine for my Outlaw Art Museum collection.

The Sinners hold down an especially important section in my archives, and many productive things happened in that period, the early '90s. The downside, the dark and evil side, came out when Cochise drank a bellyful of hard liquor. For some drinkers, Jack Daniel's can come on like liquid crack. One especially dark and dangerous night, Cochise and Heavy attempted to kill two other members who wanted to quit the gang. They threw them in the East River. Cochise and Heavy both went to prison. Before Cochise was sent up the river to Sing Sing, I told him, "Cochise, don't forget, do art. Don't forget to do art."

In prison Cochise turned his life around. He earned his GED, did a four-year apprenticeship, and got his journeyperson's papers as an offset lithographic press operator. He was released on lifetime parole and returned to the neighborhood after 18 years with a mission to council youth who are at risk for getting into the gang lifestyle. There may be no more classic Satan's Sinners-style gangs in the neighborhood, but there are new kinds of associations, like the Bloods, the Crips, and the Latin Kings, which can lead to the same bad end for kids.

He and I worked together on a book that was published in 2016, *The Street Gangs of the Lower East Side*. It combines his personal story with a history of the neighborhood's gangs. Because of the book he was released from lifetime parole. I'm so proud that I have worked with him.

13 R. O. Tyler, aka Dr. Uranian

John

In 2010, Colin Moynihan wrote in the *New York Times*:

> For decades, the East Village has been home to countless avant-garde organizations and collectives, drawn to the area by its cultural vitality and low cost of living.
>
> Those days of affordability, however, appear to have largely vanished, and over the last decade or so many of the creative groups that once had a home in the East Village have moved or become defunct.
>
> The latest to announce its departure is one of the more unusual to spring up there. That group, an artists' collective and burial society called the Uranian Phalanstery and First New York Gnostic Lyceum Temple, was started in the East Village in the late 1950s by the artists Richard Oviet Tyler and Dorothea Tyler.
>
> Faced with tax liens, the group is selling the two old brick buildings on East Fourth Street near Avenue D that it has owned since 1974.

Medi Matin, director of the Phalanstery, told Moynihan that it was moving uptown to Hamilton Heights.

That was a rare mention of the Tylers in the *Times*, and a very posthumous one for Richard, who had died of cancer in 1983. (Dorothea died in 2012.) Like Lionel Ziprin, R. O. Tyler was an influential but underground figure in postwar Lower East Side culture; like Lionel, he connected people and created webs of creativity and spirituality. In Tyler's case these included music, visual arts, printing and publishing, tattooing, Eastern religion, Gnosticism, Judaism, and communalism. And more. And all at once.

Tyler was big, bearded, heavily tattooed decades before it was hip, a jolly drinker and pot smoker who could talk your ears off. (All his tattoos were done by Dorothea.) He was widely read and erudite, conversant in unusual and esoteric paths of human endeavor. For example, "Phalanstery." A very obscure word that goes back to the early 1800s and the just as obscure

Fourierist movement. Charles Fourier was a French philosopher who advocated communal societies. There were a number of Fourierist communes in America, promoted by Horace Greeley and others. Phalanstery, combining "phalanx" and "monastery," was a term they used to define them.

Fourierism was mostly played out by the middle of the 1800s. That Tyler knew and revived the term in the 20th century says something about his knowledge of arcane history. That he wedded it to "Uranian," an astrological reference to Uranus's powerful influence on creativity and innovation, and to Gnosticism, and the Greek Lyceum, and a Jewish temple, suggests a wildly eclectic and synthesizing imagination. Which seems to have been a hallmark of Lower East Side artists and intellectuals after World War II.

He was born Richard Oviet Tyler in Lansing, Michigan, in 1924. His mother was a member of the I Am movement, a successor to Theosophy and precursor of the New Age movement, founded in Chicago in the 1930s. His father was a working-class Great War veteran, possibly a sign painter. Richard fought in the Pacific in World War II, and was among the American troops occupying Japan afterward. He developed a deep interest in Japanese tattoo traditions and Asian mysticism. Returning to the U.S., he used the GI Bill to study at the Art Institute of Chicago, where he met not only Dorothea but also Claes Oldenburg.

In the late 1950s they moved to the Lower East Side, to East 4th Street between Avenues C and D. When Oldenburg showed up Tyler got him his apartment. They not only continued their friendship, but it's likely that Tyler influenced Oldenburg's famous sculptures in ways not recognized in standard art histories. Tyler's home was filled with toy guns and ray guns and plastic hamburgers, and he sold them from his pushcart (see below). Oldenburg's Store, which he opened on East 2nd Street in 1961, sold ray guns, then he converted the storefront into Ray Gun Theater. And his soft hamburgers and cheeseburgers may well have been inspired by his friend's plastic ones.

Tyler found work doing magazine illustrations for *Playboy* and elsewhere, and would teach at the School for Visual Arts and CUNY. He also helped develop Judson Gallery at Judson Memorial Church over in Greenwich Village, a center of avant-garde art and performance in the '50s and '60s. Oldenburg was there too, and Phyllis Yampolsky, and Jim Dine. Tyler played Death in Peter Schumann's 1962 *Totentanz* at Judson, Schumann's first performance in America. He'd later found Bread & Puppet Theater.

The Tylers lived in the basement of a tenement. He became the super of that building and the one next store, a yeshiva. The neighborhood was going through one of its periodic demographic shifts, from Jewish to Puerto Rican.

He may have been the Shabbos goy for the old rabbi there as well. When the rabbi died he left the building to Richard and Dorothea, with the understanding that they would maintain its tradition as some sort of religious or spiritual place. Which they did, in their own way, by making it the headquarters of the Uranian Phalanstery and First New York Gnostic Lyceum Temple.

Richard and Dorothea started the Phalanstery in 1959. Tyler named himself Dr. Uranian and Reverend Relytor; Dorothea Baer became Madame Reab. All members of the group got these backward "secret" names. Tyler's other wacky aliases include Super Omrley, Karl Tut, Dickly Mang, Dick Tau, and Easy Louie. It's a signal that as deep and wide as the Phalanstery's esoteric references were, Tyler maintained a certain playful lightness about it all. He mixed paganism and Christianity and Buddhism and astrology and Jungianism and various other religious and philosophical modes into elaborate rituals and observances. Members took LSD and other psychedelics at some events. The Phalanstery was also a funeral society; when a member died, Tyler would conduct the 49 days of the Bardo ceremony to help the soul reach reincarnation.

Tyler was, among many other things, a jazz drummer and avant-garde musicologist, and ecstatic evenings of communally improvised music were central to the Phalanstery's observances. Composer Keith Patchel likens Tyler's musical theories, which involved astrology and numerology, to John Cage's. Lee Gongwer of the Ocarina Orchestra participated in the regular Wednesday night jams in the early '80s. "It was pretty wild. It was all improv," he recalls. The late Bill Heine, another artist who was also a magician and a jazz drummer (he played with Charlie Parker), remembered that Tyler had musical instruments all over his place. "As many as thirty or more of us came over there for his Lyceum feasts, and Richard would record us playing the instruments—often people would play an instrument that they had never played before—and it sounded amazing."

Tattoo artist Michael McCabe moved to the Tylers' block in 1979, by which time it was full-on Alphabet City, looking like Berlin at the end of the war, bombed-out, dangerous, and junkie-infested. That made it very, very cheap, so it continued to attract artists who put up with the dangers for the low rents.

McCabe has written about his first encounters with Tyler and Tyler's friend and neighbor Thom deVita, a tattooist.

> They were both heavily tattooed and at the time, this was quite extraordinary. Tyler's arms were heavily tattooed and dark with

Tibetan language mantras and graphic Chinese images . . . Thom deVita was also heavily tattooed. One of his tattoos stood out to me; several large, well-drawn, black and gray-shaded skull images were tattooed across his throat. It was a very intense tattoo that set a tone for me about the no bullshit attitude of the neighborhood.

He recalls Tyler ushering him into his basement space:

We walked underneath the front steps through an old wrought iron gate to the basement door. Tyler pushed the door open and revealed a dimly lit basement hallway that was completely plastered, walls and ceiling like a collage. There were hundreds of images and words all messed together. It was shocking and I wondered if the layered images and words represented a private historical text of some kind. Tyler then opened a second door to his basement workshop . . . A quick pan of the long room revealed in the front area a letterset press, an old Lower East Side pushcart, and against the wall two dime museum gypsy fortune teller cabinet machines with dusty mannequin women behind the cabinet glass. The cabinets looked very old . . . To the right was a central room area with a long desk, dusty bookshelves and hundreds more images and words on every surface . . .

McCabe perceptively notes:

As the creative founder of his Uranian Phalanstery, Tyler drew on his knowledge of ancient history, semiology, art history and religious studies to create a foundation for his creative masterwork. The texts on the bookshelf next to his workshop desk spoke of Tyler's influences: Carl Jung, Blavatsky, Karl Marx, Dubuffet, William Burroughs and other Beat writers; Genet, Herbert Asbury and *The Gangs of New York*. I came to understand that Tyler represented a historical link to the days of bohemian culture in the East Village and how that 1940s and 50s culture transitioned to Ginsberg, Giorno and Burroughs. Values of outsiderism, criminality as a liberating alternative and counterculturism were operative theories of life. What was then the totally ignored and privatized world of the East Village and the Lower East Side was a haven for people who didn't give a shit about the mundane and arcane life of "civilians." At that time in 1979, life east of First Avenue to the river operated on its own terms and values.

The practice of tattooing had not yet been accepted as a viable and integral art form. During the 1970s, even in a place like the East Village, having a tattoo was associated with odd, untrusting behavior; a criminal or deviant life. There was nothing trendy about the practice. It scared people. Tyler adopted tattooing as one of his pursuits because of the visceral communicative appeal but also because it was connected to outsider values—a no turning back from a commitment to those outsider values.

Tyler's tattoo art was decades ahead of the curve. He was influenced by yakuza tattoos and other Pacific and African traditions well before the 1989 *Modern Primitives* ushered in the era of tribal tats. At a time when much tattoo design came from commercial "flash," he was personally designing tattoos to fit the tattooee. As in most everything he did, he added layers of the mystical and magical. Jungian archetypes and astrological signs played roles in the choice of designs and symbols. Most remarkably, he acquired esoteric compounds from the Dalai Lama's apothecary, substances like crushed pearls that had mystical and medicinal uses in Tibetan practice, and mixed them with his tattoo ink.

Tyler was a master woodblock artist. McCabe recalls, "After an initial meeting with Tyler where the tattoo designs were discussed and chosen, he would use his master woodcutting skills to carve woodblocks of the small symbols or images. These were then used like ink stamps, much the way traditional Thai tattooers use wooden stamps to transfer their tattoo images to the body."

Under the rubric of his Uranian Press, Tyler wrote, illustrated, printed, and distributed a stream of pamphlets, booklets, broadsheets, astrological calendars, photocopied collages, and lithographs. This is where the pushcart comes in. Tyler loaded it up in his basement and trundled it over to just outside Judson Church, where he or a designated backward-named Uranian would sell items on the cheap. Matin curated a display of them at Printed Matter in 2017. Densely packing hand-lettered words and woodcut images, they're mysterious, mystical, profane, comical—all at once.

Although Tyler lives in the memories and on the skins of the many people he influenced and inked, the Uranian Press materials may represent the most permanent record of his personal multiverse. Maybe someday somebody in the art world will study them and assign Tyler a more visible place in the history of downtown Manhattan culture in the decades after World War II, when New York was, for a time, the art capital of the world, and the Lower East Side was one of its busier quarters.

14 Molly Picon

John

John originally wrote this for *The Chiseler*.

The Yiddish theaters that thrived on and near 2nd Avenue from the 1880s until around Word War II played a huge role in the culture of the Lower East Side. They had a big influence on world culture as well, not least through Hollywood movies, where a number of actors and directors were former 2nd Avenue stars.

In her day, Molly Picon was one of the best known of them.

. . .

Molly Picon stopped growing when she was a kid and topped out at around four foot eight—four-eleven standing on her tiptoes, she liked to say. The biggest thing about her was her impish Betty Boop eyes. But she packed a lot of energy and spirit into that miniature package. She could and would do anything to amuse an audience—sing, dance, do a somersault, climb a rope, crack jokes, wear blackface or boy's knickers. She played gamins, waifs, soubrettes well into her matronly years. The one thing she wouldn't and maybe couldn't do was to hide or even just tone down her essential Jewishness to appeal to the goys in the mainstream audience. It sets her apart from many other Jewish entertainers of her day. Whether she was performing in Yiddish or English, on 2nd Avenue or in Hollywood, there was never any question that Molly Picon was Jewish. Very Jewish.

She was born Malka Pyekoon on the Lower East Side in 1898, in a fourth-floor back bedroom of a tenement on Broome Street near Bowery. Her mother was a seamstress who'd escaped the pogroms near Kiev as one of a dozen children. Her father was an educated man from Warsaw who was never happy doing an immigrant's menial labor in America, so he did as little as he could. He also turned out to have a previous wife back in

Poland he'd never legally divorced. He drifted in and mostly out of Molly and her sister Helen's lives. Decades later, when Molly became well-off and world famous, he'd drift back into hers, to borrow money.

Their mother and grandmother picked up and moved the girls to Philadelphia, where Mom became a seamstress at a Yiddish theater and took in boarders. Later she'd run a small grocery store. The story of how Molly got her start in show business—like many of the tales in her charming and irrepressibly schmaltzy memoir *Molly!*—is too good not to be true. When Molly was 5 her mother, who made all her daughters' clothes out of odds and ends, stitched her up a fine outfit and took her on a trolley headed for amateur night at a burlesque theater, the Bijou. On the trolley a drunk challenged the little girl to show him her act. She sang and danced in the aisle. Charmed, he passed the hat and collected two dollars. At the Bijou the audience tossed pennies on the stage while she performed. She also won the first prize, a $5 gold piece. Her grandmother was astonished at the $10 she'd earned—roughly a week's wages for an adult worker. When her mother said she was going to start taking her around to all the amateur contests, her grandmother said forget the theaters, there weren't enough in Philadelphia—just keep taking her on the trolley.

Mike Thomashefsky, brother of Boris (then king of the 2nd Avenue scene), ran Philadelphia's Columbia Theatre. Mike soon put Molly and Helen in a Yiddish production of *Uncle Tom's Cabin*, Helen as Little Eva, Molly in blackface as Topsy. Molly, billed as Baby Margaret, continued to act through her childhood. She dropped out of high school in 1915 to tour small-time vaudeville in a female quartet, the Four Seasons. In Boston in 1918 she visited a Yiddish theater group who performed one night a week at the Grand Opera House, which staged wrestling and boxing the rest of the week. One of the young actors she met there was Muni Weisenfreund, who had come to the Lower East Side from Galicia at the age of 5, already acting. Later, under the name Paul Muni, he'd become one of the three great gangsters of pre-Code Hollywood, in *Scarface*.

Jacob Kalich, who ran the Boston theater company, came like Weisenfreund from Galicia, a province in the Austro-Hungarian empire. He'd studied to be a rabbi but then fell in with traveling Yiddish theater troupes. He'd slipped into America without a passport and speaking no English in 1914. Kalich hired Molly away from the Seasons; they fell in love and were married the next year in the back room of her mother's grocery store. According to Molly's memoir, her mother stitched her wedding gown from a stage curtain.

Yonkel, as Molly called Kalich, wrote parts and whole plays specifically for his new wife. One was *Yonkele*, an operetta in which she wore boys' clothes and sang, danced, and did her somersaults as a kind of Yiddish Dennis the Menace. After a child was stillborn in 1920 Kalich distracted Molly with a new project. They sailed for Europe. His plan was to make her a star (and improve her Yiddish) in the theaters there, then return in triumph. They started in Paris, where *Yonkele* was a hit, then toured it around Europe for two years. She made her first Yiddish-themed silent films in Vienna starting in 1921, playing a sassy soubrette or a boy. When they were in Bucharest hundreds of university students shouting anti-Semitic slurs rioted in and outside of a theater where she was performing. It was time to come home.

Jews around Europe had been writing their American relations about the wonderful new star. By 1922 the 2nd Avenue Theatre near East 2nd Street was happy to host *Yonkele* and anything else Kalich put together, as long as it had Picon in it—*Gypsy Girl*, *The Circus Girl*, *Schmendrick*, *Oy is dus a Madel* (Oh, What a Girl!). Picon played to houses packed not just with Yiddish-speaking Lower East Siders but with celebrities like Greta Garbo, Mayor Jimmy Walker, Albert Einstein, and D. W. Griffith. Griffith was on the downside of a long career by then and tried, without success, to raise money for a film starring Picon. Flo Ziegfeld and his wife Billie Burke (the good witch in *Wizard of Oz*) came over from Broadway to see Molly perform. Afterward, Yonkel and Molly took them to a Jewish restaurant, where the waiter covered the table with plates of pickles, sauerkraut, fried steak, radishes slathered in schmaltz. The very goy Burke asked the waiter if she might have some vegetables. What, he snorted, pickles and sauerkraut aren't vegetables?

Picon was such a star that Kalich got the idea of renaming the theater the Molly Picon Theatre. When their packed performance schedule there permitted, they toured Yiddish theaters around the country. Later, Jews who had fled Eastern Europe for South America organized a tour for her there. She would also tour South Africa.

She returned to vaudeville in a big way, headlining at the grand Palace in Times Square with Sophie Tucker. Picon sang half her songs in English, Tucker sang half of hers in Yiddish, and they triumphed. When Picon played the Palace in Chicago, Al Capone (who had started out on the Lower East Side himself) bought out the first three rows. After the show he took Picon and Kalich out to dinner. At his request she sang "The Rabbi's Melody" (a big hit on 2nd Avenue) and, she claims, he "cried like a baby." For the rest of her career she introduced it as "the song that made Al Capone cry."

The crash of 1929 ruined Picon and Kalich along with everybody else. They scrambled to get back on their feet. They took over the lush Yiddish Art Theatre on 2nd Avenue and renamed it Molly Picon's Folks Theatre. In 1936 she and Yonkel sailed back to Europe to film a Yiddish musical in Poland, *Yidl mitn Fidl* (Yidl with a Fiddle). She plays a penniless girl who disguises herself as a boy to join a band of traveling musicians. Location shooting took place in Kazimierz, the once grand, now bedraggled Jewish zone in Krakow. They recruited the whole neighborhood as extras for a big wedding scene that took days to shoot. Few if any of the locals, deeply Orthodox and very poor, had ever seen a movie. They marveled at the food that kept appearing as scenes of the wedding feast were shot and reshot.

Yidl was a hit with Yiddish audiences worldwide. It inspired one of Hollywood's great eccentrics, director Edgar G. Ulmer, to shoot a couple of his own Yiddish films in America. Ulmer, another Jewish immigrant from the Austro-Hungarian empire, had started his career in Hollywood directing the 1934 Karloff-Lugosi vehicle *The Black Cat* for Carl Laemmle's Universal Pictures. When he saw *Yidl* drawing big crowds on 2nd Avenue he started a small Yiddish production company, Collective Film Producers, and filmed *Grine Felder* (Green Fields), re-creating the shtetl in a field in New Jersey on a shoestring budget. Ulmer spoke no Yiddish himself, so he hired the 2nd Avenue star Jacob Ben-Ami as co-director and go-between with the cast of 2nd Avenue actors. The movie went on to be one of the most praised in the history of Yiddish film.

As the 1930s drew to a close, Picon and Kalich saw that they were playing to the same dwindling and aging audiences over and over. Yiddish was dying out among the American-born children of immigrants, taking Yiddish theater with it. Although they would continue to work on 2nd Avenue through the 1950s, Picon still playing Yonkele in her fifties, it was clear they needed to work harder to crack the mainstream.

In 1942 she returned to Broadway with a big gamble, her and Yonkel's musical *Oy Is Dus a Leben!* (Oh Is This a Life!), the first Yiddish play on Broadway. It was a vanity piece about Molly's life and their marriage, and they played themselves on stage. The Al Jolson Theatre was renamed the Molly Picon Theatre for the occasion. The show ran for a respectable 17 weeks, and she claims it only ended when the producers, feeling that they'd shown it to every Jew in New York by then, decided to quit while they were ahead.

During World War Two Picon did many U.S.O. concerts, played every military base she could get to, and joined in many all-star benefits for refugees. She stands out in a very brief and uncredited scene in *The Naked City*, the 1948 cop movie inspired by Weegee's book. After that, while she remained very busy on stage and did some tv, there was nothing much from Hollywood until 1963, when she played Frank Sinatra's mom in the screen version of Neil Simon's *Come Blow Your Horn*. When Frank had signed on they changed Simon's Jewish family to Italian to accommodate him. Then they hired Picon and changed it back to Jewish. It's not a good movie but it was a box office success and Picon earned an Oscar nomination for her performance.

Fiddler on the Roof opened on Broadway in 1964. It was a record-setting hit that ran until July 1972. Remarkably, Picon was not in it. The role of Yente the matchmaker went to Bea Arthur. But when Norman Jewison—not himself Jewish, despite the name—put together the cast for the 1971 film adaptation, he studied *Yidl mitn Fidl* for background and hired Picon.

After Yonkel died in 1975 she gradually withdrew from the public eye, puttering around in their home up the Hudson, which they'd named Chez Schmendrick. She wrote her memoir, did a little more tv (Grandma Mona on *The Facts of Life*) and a couple more movies (Mrs. Goldfarb in *The Cannonball Run* and *Cannonball Run II*), and in 1979 toured a one-woman show, *Hello, Molly!* But her own health was deteriorating. She lived her last decade quietly and was 92 when she died in 1992.

15 LA II

Clayton

LA II should have been one of the most famous artists to come out of the Lower East Side in recent decades. As a collaborator with Keith Haring, LA II has struck as deep into the American artscape as Haring did. LA II was instrumental in pushing Haring from being just a graphic artist to a full-on fine artist. They did years of work together. Yet his contribution to Haring's art has often gone undervalued or entirely uncredited by museums and art historians.

He was born in 1967 and grew up in the Baruch public housing complex. He was tagging by the age of 10 as LA II (for Little Angel). After Keith saw LA II's work—Angel was 13 at the time—he sought him and asked him to collaborate with him. Keith did his graphics and LA II did the filling flow between the graphics with his signature *LA II*. The two working in tandem turned Keith's designs into art.

Haring was a nerdy, gay, small-town white boy when he came to the big city. According to *Keith Haring's Line: Race and Performance of Desire*, by Richard Montez, Haring needed a comfort zone that he found by dealing with people from a lower class than his own. It raises the issues of insecurities and white power. It's one of the reasons I think LA II was important to Haring. It is my belief that LA II was a security blanket. Haring was young, having his first experiences in the art world, working on shows and projects sponsored by sophisticated art world people. That had to be somewhat frightening. The pressure had to have been made more bearable with LA II as his partner. A working partner, a minority from a lower class, locked into the same art/work zone, including the trips abroad, which must also have been intimidating to the boy from Kutztown, PA.

Montez also describes Haring's insatiable appetite for inner-city black and Hispanic lovers. LA II was Hispanic, but not gay. Still, he did have street cred in the ghetto. He could get Keith safe passage to the hood, the projects, and even the train yards. The street and graffiti were important to Keith. He fronted his relationship to both. Meeting young, inner-city, low-income Hispanic males was one of his drives. In those days wandering around the Lower East Side was not something most people from outside were comfortable doing. It was extremely dangerous to do. All the streets had an open and active hard drug market. LA II got Keith a pass to tag in the neighborhood. I interviewed the person who ran the CBS street crew and the heroin on a number of blocks on Avenue D. He gave Keith a pass. This is why Keith was able to do the CBS crew DJ Robot mural on Avenue D by Houston Street.

The act of erasing LA II started with Haring's very first solo show in 1982. LA II's work was a major part of this show. Not a mention. He was on the poster and invitation card, a cute, unnamed little brown boy. The photographer, Tseng Kwong Chi, was named. Not Angel. One art critic described this as being in vogue at the time, showing the "noble savage" in art. He was referring to Basquiat and Angel Ortiz.

Angel came to me for help after a Keith Haring exhibition at the Whitney Museum of American Art in 2002 gave credit only to Haring. Angel was depressed. What could I do? I gave him a show in my gallery, and got a story by Colin Moynihan into the *Village Voice* about the problem of being "Keith Haring's Silent Partner."

In 2008, the New Museum and Deitch Projects (dealer Jeffrey Deitch represents Haring's estate), to celebrate what would be Keith's 50th birthday, spent $30,000 to re-create his famous 1982 mural at Houston and Bowery. Angel and I walked up to Houston with a ladder, and he added his work to the reproduction, making it a Keith Haring and LA II collaborative work of art, just like the old days.

This time it made the *New York Times*. Fab Five Freddy told the *Times*, "I think Keith would have loved it. Back then Keith was looking for influences and inspiration, and he got a great deal of it from LA II's work."

Soon after this, LA showed me an umbrella from Pop Shop. The design on the fabric was only LA II's work, but again it was being sold as Haring's.

At the Brooklyn Museum's 2012 Keith Haring exhibition, Angel Ortiz was just a name on a list of artists Keith had collaborated with, including Basquiat and Kenny Scharf. This was just smudging art history. Yes, maybe Haring collaborated with those others in small ways, but his one true art collaboration was with Angel Ortiz. Their collaborations are as tightly woven together as a Navaho blanket.

Angel's work was in the Whitney Museum's memorial show right after Keith died—but his name was not. The Whitney's *Keith Haring* book is saturated with examples of unattributed LA II/Haring collaborations. The book is so damaging because it is an educational tool. One can pore over it for hours, compare and contrast images, go back to it as often as one wants. A museum visitor does not have the same opportunity to study the work. Just as with ancient hieroglyphics, people study the iconography of the images in this book to become Haring "experts." As it happens, there is one photo in the book of LA II working with Haring, on the 1983 sarcophagus. This photograph can give the impression LA II was just a work-for-hire assistant. Jeffrey Deitch, Haring's dealer, explicitly said to me that LA II's work with Haring was work-for-hire, not a collaboration.

How differently would the art establishment have treated LA II if he was not a Puerto Rican from the projects on the Lower East Side? How is the way he was treated not racist? After 20 years of our demanding answers to these questions, he finally started to get a bit of the credit he had always deserved. Things may be improving now, in the light of the Black Lives Matter movement. But until recently, if you were a poor, brown artist from the Lower East Side, you had to work hard and long for your value to be recognized by the art world.

16 Al and Angel Orensanz

John

Nowhere do the roots of the American Jewish community run deeper or broader than on the Lower East Side.

The handsome Neo-Gothic synagogue at 172 Norfolk Street that's now home to the Angel Orensanz Foundation is said to be the oldest standing synagogue in America. It was built in 1848–49 by the German immigrant Anshe Chesed congregation, one of the first Reform congregations in the country. They had begun as an Orthodox congregation in the 1820s and previously worshipped in a former Quaker meetinghouse down on Henry Street in what's now Chinatown. In 1848 they bought property on Norfolk Street between Houston and Stanton Streets and hired a German architect to design the synagogue, which he did in the Gothic style with high arches, a lofty vaulted ceiling, and beautiful wooden pews and choir lofts, effectively indistinguishable from a Christian church. When it opened it could seat 1,500, making it the largest synagogue in America at the time.

Anshe Chesed moved uptown in the 1870s. Over the next century, one congregation after another took over the Norfolk Street building. As the German Reform Jews moved uptown, Eastern European Orthodox congregations moved in. By the 1970s they had moved on as well, and in 1974 the building stood abandoned and boarded up. All of which reflects changes the whole neighborhood went through in the 19th and 20th centuries. Wave after wave of new immigrants arriving, striving, moving on, abandoning the area.

But the synagogue's story takes a unique turn. For a decade after it went empty in the mid-1970s the fine old building deteriorated, its beautiful wooden pews broken up by vandals, its Gothic arches and vaulted ceiling perches for prolifically defecating pigeons. The roof was falling in, the floor buckling, the facade crumbling. By the mid-1980s the city had posted it as unsafe, a bureaucratic step toward demolition. As one history of the building put it, "it was just a block and a lot number in the city's rolls, part of a neighborhood burnt down and boarded-up."

That's when a new immigrant saw it and recognized its potential. Angel Orensanz had just come to New York. He'd grown up in a Sephardic Jewish home in the autonomous region of Aragon in northern Spain. (It's worth noting that Sephardic Jews were the first in New Amsterdam, in the 1650s.) He was a sculptor and painter who had the kind of faith in himself and his art that some of the neighborhood's more self-effacing artists could have used a pinch of. (For example, see the chapters in this volume on Lionel Ziprin and John Evans.) When he peered in through the dusty windows, he saw a potentially glorious space where he could work and exhibit his art. He and his devoted older brother Al, a Ph.D. sociologist who had immigrated to New York years earlier, bought the building and rechristened it for Angel. With extensive repairs and renovation they brought it back from a decrepit wreck to its original status as a neighborhood landmark and cultural jewel.

Besides showing Angel's work, the space developed into an impressive cultural center, run by Al and his work partner Maria Neri. In a span of three decades they brought an impressive and eclectic array of cultural luminaries to the synagogue to exhibit their art, perform, or give talks. A very partial list would include Gerry Adams of Sinn Fein, Philip Glass (who lives in the neighborhood), Lady Gaga, and Lou Reed (each of whom lived in the neighborhood for a few years), film director Sidney Lumet (who grew up there), Elie Wiesel, Norman Mailer, Alicia Keys, Whitney Houston, Jacques Derrida, E. L. Doctorow, Steve Martin, art historian Thomas McEvelly (who lived on East 2nd Street, and described the building as "an ancient spirit with folded wings on a little traveled block of Norfolk St."), the Royal Shakespeare Company, the Wooster Group, Arthur Miller, Al Pacino, the Kronos Quartet, and early performances of Benjamin Bagby's celebrated *Beowulf* in Old English. In 1999 a boxing ring was set up for a match between the writer/performer Jonathan Ames, boxing as "The Herring Wonder," and David "The Impact Artist" Leslie. The band Gov't Mule released their album *Live at the Angel Orensanz Center* in 2008.

It was like the downtown Carnegie Hall and 92nd Street Y combined. It was also the setting for lavish weddings, high holiday services conducted by the Shul of New York (self-described as a "liberal non-denominational synagogue"), fundraisers for local groups like the Lower East Side Girls Club, and the first New York Acker Awards celebration. An estimated one million people went through the doors over those thirty years.

Al Orensanz died in 2016. He was 74. Ed Litvak wrote:

Al Orensanz served as director of the center for the past 30 years. He was a sociologist and published author. In the past few years, he was working on a novel about the working class and immigrants in Brooklyn in the 1990s. Orensanz was also nearly finished with a history book about the Norfolk Street building and its relationship to the always-changing Lower East Side. But in the neighborhood, he'll always be remembered for those heroic efforts to save the former synagogue from the wrecking ball.

In a period when so many places for culture were vanishing all over the Lower East Side, the Orensanzes and Neri offered a counterexample that not only preserved a legacy but began a new one.

17 John Evans

John

John wrote this as the introduction to the book *1984: Collages by John Evans*, published by the Quantuck Lane Press in 2011.

. . .

Sioux Falls, South Dakota, at the tail end of the Depression years seems an unlikely place and time for a boy to learn art. Yet that's where John Evans, born on August 24, 1932, took his first art lessons when he was "maybe 7 or 8." A classmate's mother who'd studied at the Art Institute of Chicago taught him. When he was an adolescent his family moved to Redondo Beach, California; he remembers a long drive across the desert and his father having to fill the radiator with coffee from a thermos when they ran out of water. His father was an electrician, his mother a nurse, and John was the eldest of their five children. As a teenager in Southern California, he says, just about the only art he saw was religious images and the macho tattoos he and other guys got in high school.

In more than one way those humble beginnings have carried through Evans's career as an artist. After serving stateside in the army during the Korean War, he went to the Art Institute on the GI Bill and in 1963 earned an MFA. From there he went straight to New York City, then the art capital of the world. Still, he seems to have lacked the self-promotional gene that made some of his contemporaries stars of the art market. He tends to speak of his paintings and collages offhandedly as "what I do" and takes a nonchalant approach to storing a prodigious output that would give any archivist the willies. Even the materials he works with are humble. Not to put too fine a point on it, he makes art from other people's trash.

From 1964 through 2000 Evans collected flotsam and jetsam that caught his eye on the streets around his Lower East Side apartment. He picked up playing cards, tarot cards, holy cards, business cards, ticket stubs, candy cigarette packs, fortune cookie fortunes, leaflets advertising rock bands and escort services, shreds of fabric, and labels for products such as Cry Baby Table Grapes, Darkie Tooth Paste, Fitrite ("the Underwear of Modesty"), and Korrect Shape Shoes. He pocketed buttons, beads, dice, keys, subway tokens. He gathered paranoid political flyers, scraps of newspapers and magazines, ripped-up snapshots, canceled stamps, savings stamps, liquor and wine labels, matchbooks ("Pince Nez Safety Matches"), wrapping paper, photobooth strips, antique portrait gallery shots, cardboard containers for poisons like Liquor Cresolis Compositus and Hi-Resilience Carbamate, postcards, scrawled letters and notes (part of a bizarre letter about a mummy's hand, a note posted at Leo Castelli's gallery altered to read "PLEASE CLOSE DOOR WHEN EXCITING, THANK-YOU.").

Every day for 37 years, except for a day he felt too sick (February 11, 1996, to be precise), Evans sat in his apartment with a sketchbook, turned to the next blank page, and arranged some of this discarded ephemera into a collage. Often he would include something of his own, like his humorous business card or photos of himself or of his twin daughters, Honor and India, born in 1978. Then he rubber-stamped the day's date on it. By the end of 2000 he had created more than twelve thousand collages, filling more than a hundred sketchbooks, which he crammed into bookshelves and trunks.

Most of the time Evans made his collages in sketchbooks with pages of $8\frac{1}{2} \times 11$ inches. In 1984 a woman he knew who worked in the college textbook division at McGraw-Hill gave him a couple of dummy books with blank pages of 5×7 inches. He filled them with collages, then went back to working in the larger sketchbooks. Although the dimensions differ, the style and methodology used here are consistent with his collages from other years. All the images in *1984* are from that year. Any parallels the viewer might see between this *1984* and George Orwell's, Evans says, are accidental.

Writing in the *New York Times* in 1976, Hilton Kramer likened Evans's collages to Joseph Cornell's boxes, but they're less precious and hermetic than that. The Dadaist Kurt Schwitters, whose collages engaged the viewer and the world more aggressively, seems a better reference point. Evans—who expresses little interest in how he's labeled—has been called a neo-dadaist, and rubber-stamped neologisms such as LOISAIDADA (*Loisaida*, the Puerto Rican name for the Lower East Side, plus *dada*) turn up in his work.

As you page through the images in *1984* and in the 2005 monograph *John Evans: Collages*, several layers of meaning suggest themselves. On one level Evans's collages comprise a pictorial diary of his personal and family life. You can spot his mood shifts from bright ebullience to dark and brooding. You see his hair turn gray and vanish altogether, check in periodically on Honor and India as they grow up, track his gallery exhibitions through invitations and reviews. There are tributes, sometimes coded and enigmatic, to his friends and neighbors over the years. His politics come through on occasion ("EVICT REAGAN IN 1984"), his sense of humor often.

On another level, as assemblages of what his neighbors threw away, these images add up to a mosaic portrait of the East Village and Lower East Side in all their funky, shabby-chic, polyglot glory. And because all the world came to the Lower East Side, they have a way of expanding to evoke a global perspective, if a wry and somewhat skewed one. Finally, for those familiar with the neighborhood, these pages resonate with both history and nostalgia. The neighborhood went through waves of change across the decades when Evans was enshrining its castoffs. Today his neighbors are more likely to be wealthy professionals than the artists and working-class immigrants whose lives are conjured in fragments here. It's noteworthy that the New-York Historical Society, recognizing that Evans's work is filled with glimpses of a vanishing neighborhood culture, hosted an exhibition of his collages in 2002.

. . .

Like many young artists, Evans arrived in New York and went straight to the Lower East Side because the rents there were very cheap. His first apartment, on Avenue B near East 6th Street, was $35 a month. He has been in his current apartment, a third-floor walk-up in an old tenement in East 3rd Street, since the early 1970s. The rent there started at $63 and is still under $200. The rooms are small and spare but high-ceilinged, with good light through the windows. The stairs up from the street level are marble, worn concave by a century of tramping feet. There's no buzzer at the street door; visitors phone from downstairs and Evans or his wife, Margaret, throws down a key. They raised Honor and India there. "They're real LES girls," he says. Both still live in New York, where India, who lived in Italy for five years, makes collages of her own.

"When I first came here it was like Europe," he recalls. "It was really Old World. There were enclaves of Italians and Jews and Poles and Ukrainians. There were still pushcarts on Avenue C, people selling thread and things like that. It was strange to me, coming from California." His first landlord ran Izzy's Luncheonette on the ground floor below his apartment; his much longer-term landlord is Chinese.

Evans has worked a variety of jobs to supplement his income as an artist. He drove a cab, tended bar, cut mats for an art gallery, and until recently watered the plants in Manhattan offices three days a week. His first job in New York was for the Metropolitan Museum of Art, where young artists sat at long tables, opening mail and processing orders for the museum's line of Christmas cards. It was called the "quarter mail" because people mailed a quarter for the catalogue. One day he saw "a scrap of paper with a guy's face on it in the waste basket. It almost said, 'Use me.' That became his first collage." He always carried a sketchbook with him and began to fill one up with collages, but he says he did not intend at first to make it the daily routine it became.

The mail room was in a leased space at 980 Madison Avenue, where Gagosian Gallery is today. On the floor above was the Cordier & Ekstrom Gallery, begun in 1959 by Arne Ekstrom. Along with exhibiting work by older avant-gardists including Duchamp and Man Ray (with catalogue texts by authors the likes of Octavio Paz, Donald Barthelme, and Margaret Mead), Ekstrom encouraged new artists.

"I would go see his shows," Evans recalls. "One day I walked in with a sketchbook and he asked to see it." Ekstrom showed it to one of his gallery's artists, Alfonso Ossorio, known for his own found-object assemblages (and for being a friend and collector of Jackson Pollock), who bought it for $500. "I was just out of art school. Five hundred dollars seemed fine," Evans says. Ekstrom later took Evans on as one of his artists. The collages Hilton Kramer reviewed in 1976 were in a group show at Ekstrom's gallery, where Evans would get his first major solo exhibition in 1980. (He has showed at several other galleries in the city since. For roughly the past decade he has exhibited at Pavel Zoubok Gallery in Chelsea, where India now also shows.)

From the late 1960s on Evans painted watercolor backgrounds for the collages, from eye-popping yellows and oranges to muddy grays, often in two colors to suggest a horizon. A frieze of ducks' heads usually peers at (or, more pointedly, almost dismissively, away from) the viewer from behind this horizon. He called them Ursuline ducks, a tribute to the artist and writer Ursule Molinaro, one of his first New York friends. She depicted ducks and other folk artish animals in her own Haitian-inspired work, including a pair of painted chests in Evans's home. He contributed collages and she wrote text for a short collaborative book, *Remnants of an Unknown Woman*, published in 1987. He continued to incorporate the Ursuline ducks in his work almost until Molinaro's death in 2000.

The mail artist Ray Johnson also appears in various ways in Evans's art. They met at a party in Greenwich Village in 1964. Noticing Evans's high school tattoo, a dagger on his left forearm, Ray left the room and came back with a drawing of a knife that still hangs, framed, in Evans's apartment. Through Johnson, Evans got involved in the international mail art movement, references to which crop up often in the collages. To this day the John Evans Fan Club—mail art friends in California—circulates "fake John Evans" collages collectively composed by mail artists around the world; the last artist in line mails the finished product to Evans, who has binders fat with them. He and Johnson remained friends until the latter's death, a probable suicide, in 1995.

A more obscure artist, G. Berkowitz, lived below Evans's Avenue B apartment in the 1960s. "He was this little, birdlike man, probably in his 70s. He always wore a suit and tie and a little fedora. I didn't know what he did. I'd see him in the hall and say hello, but we never became friendly." When Berkowitz died, his apartment was found to be filled with his own folk art paintings. Evans saved two of them and believes the new tenants threw the rest out. He modeled his own business card ("JOHN EVANS, M.F.A., AVENUE B SCHOOL OF ART") on Berkowitz's, which had an artist's palette in the corner above "G. BERKOWITZ, ARTIST."

Around 1980, Evans rescued another artwork from possible oblivion. He was walking his daughters, "one on my back in a backpack and one in a stroller," to a nearby day-care center. On East 4th Street he saw a painting leaning up against a hot dog vendor's cart and recognized it as *Ian and Mary*, a portrait by his friend Alice Neel from 1971. The vendor offered it to him for $15—exactly the amount Evans had in his pocket. He took it home and called Neel, whom he'd known since the late 1960s; she'd painted his portrait and a famous nude of Margaret pregnant. She told him *Ian and Mary* had been stolen and asked if he'd bring it right to her. "I said, 'Well, as a matter of fact I was hoping we could negotiate an exchange.' She was like, 'Grrr.'" She gave in and he traded her *Ian and Mary* for a warm, funny portrait of Margaret playing with the twins.

. . .

The images in *1984* take on their historical or nostalgic luster in light of what was happening to the neighborhood in 1984 and after. As Evans made his rounds through the 1960s and 1970s, obsessively collecting what others tossed out, it was losing the Old World charm that had at first mystified him. It deteriorated into the harder, meaner Alphabet City, where drug gangs and violent hoodlums ruled the streets. Landlords cut services and abandoned buildings to heroin addicts and squatters or burned them down for the insurance, until the neighborhood was so pockmarked with rubble-strewn lots it looked like London or Berlin after World War II.

One day toward the end of the 1960s Evans was coming in the door of the Avenue B building with his arms full of groceries when a young man accosted him with a knife. Evans had $5 in his pocket, which he gave over, and the mugger left. Evans went into Izzy's Luncheonette.

"Johnny, you look so pale!" Izzy cried.

"Well, I just got mugged in your hall," Evans replied.

"Sit down. Let me give you a seltzer," Izzy said.

Cops caught the mugger but Evans declined to press charges.

By 1984 the neighborhood was changing yet again. It was still drug-infested and bombed-out, but signs of upscaling gentrification were noticeable enough to prompt a *New York* magazine cover story that May. Pioneering developers were making surprising plans to buy the Christodora, a 16-story art deco tower from the 1920s near Tompkins Square Park, and turn it into luxury condominiums. Originally a settlement house providing numerous services to the neighborhood's poor, it had decayed into a city-owned hulk in the 1970s, used by the local chapter of the Black Panthers as their headquarters and as a film studio by pornographers. In the summer of 1988, when phalanxes of baton-swinging cops would battle antigentrification protesters in what came to be known as the Tompkins Square Park police riot, the protesters would lay siege to the swankily renovated Christodora and drag potted trees out of the lobby for symbolic replanting in the park.

An explosion of small new art galleries including Fun and Gracie Mansion—more than 50 of them by 1984—was sparking the short-lived but hectic punk and graffiti art scene from which Keith Haring, Jean-Michel Basquiat, and Kenny Scharf emerged. Evans would exhibit a 25-year retrospective of his collages at Gracie Mansion in 1990. Funky-chic boutiques, bistros, and art bars like Pyramid and Red Bar were sprouting everywhere. Evans tended bar during this period at the Tompkins Square Restaurant, known to locals as the Pharmacy because previously "it had been a drugstore that got busted because they were selling, you know, *drugs*."

Through the 1990s, with the slogan "Die Yuppie Scum!" stenciled on sidewalks and walls throughout the neighborhood, the vibrant cultural and social life attracted more and more affluent newcomers to what was once a no-man's-land to anyone who could afford to avoid it. The pace of the upscale colonizing only accelerated in the general housing boom of the 2000s. Sleek new condo towers rose among the tenements. CBGB, birthplace of punk rock and one of the neighborhood's defining institutions, closed and was replaced by a boutique selling $500 sweaters. Even the Hells Angels clubhouse not far from Evans's apartment acquired new, well-heeled neighbors. ("Our building is worth millions and we get offers every 5 fucking minutes," an Angel told me in 2008. "Me, I'd rather die here, burn the fucking building down before I sell it.")

An apartment across the street from Evans's, of comparable size, fetches rent more than twenty times what he pays. There are still rough and funky patches in the neighborhood, but even the more downbeat blocks of Avenue B around the corner from Evans's home are now dotted with shiny new boîtes.

"It's become chic to live here," he says, laughing in wonder. "I don't get it. It's cheaper now on the Upper East Side," Manhattan's traditional enclave for the wealthy.

Maybe it's fitting that Evans stopped making his collages at the end of 2000, before this wave of change built into a tsunami. Asked about the timing of this decision in 2004, he said, "It's like when you're doing a painting, you have to know when to quit. I thought the end of the 20th century seemed like a perfect time to not be doing this anymore. Now that it's been a while, I think maybe I'll start painting again. But it's sort of nice not to. I'm kind of lazy."

A few years after he said that, Evans was diagnosed with acquired hydrocephalus, a buildup of fluids on the brain. The condition disrupts his brain's communication with his legs. After decades of walking all over the city he was reduced to shuffling baby steps and a cane.

"It's not painful, it's just a drag," he says. "Just walking to Avenue A is a chore." But he still picks up scraps and small objects that catch his eye along the way. "I can't stop," he admits with a chuckle. "It's ridiculous."

In 2011 he started making collages again. "But not one every day," he notes. "Just when I feel like it."

. . .

John's health did not improve. He passed away in 2012.

The Hells Angels sold their clubhouse on East 3rd Street in 2019.

Afterword

In the late 1990s, I went to the Vatican at Lionel Ziprin's request. Lionel came from the ancient Abulafia family of rabbis of the town of Safed in Galilee. Abraham Abulafia, who taught the Kabbalah in the 13th century, went to Rome in 1280 intending to convert Pope Nicholas III to Judaism. The Pope has him thrown in jail and wants him burned at the stake as a heretic. But then the Pope dies that very night. The people of Rome are very frightened and free Abulafia to go on his way. Come forward seven centuries, and Lionel's grandfather Rabbi Abulafia journeys to the Lower East Side.

In the early 1990s I introduced Lionel to John, and John wrote his two articles about him for *NYPress*, chapters 2 and 3 in this book. In 1995 I started going to Europe for the annual Wildstyle festival. Lionel asks me to go to the Vatican for him on one of these trips and and get John's articles into the Vatican archive. Sure, why not? I'm not Catholic, I have no connections in the Vatican, the only priest I know is Father Pat (chapter 9), and he's in prison for the Brinks robbery. But I'll try.

As it happens, I was getting a lot of dental work done at the time, which included implanting gold teeth. You know who else had gold teeth? R. O. Tyler. He was following the magical tradition that a man with gold teeth cannot tell a lie. The dentist who made my gold teeth was in Rome. Her office is right by the Vatican library and archive. She's the dentist for the priest who publishes the Pope's documents. So she takes me over and introduces me to him. He got me the passes to enter the archive and take John's articles to the right person there.

So John's articles about Lionel that were in *NYPress*, a weekly newspaper in New York City, are in the Vatican archive. Lionel wanted them there because of the medieval Abulafia family connection, and Lionel had a way of making the unlikely happen. It's classic Lower East Side magic. And now they're part of this book, and, I hope, part of you.

—Clayton

www.ingramcontent.com/pod-product-compliance
Lightning Source LLC
Chambersburg PA
CBHW070054120526
44588CB00033B/1424